国家出版基金项目
NATIONAL PUBLICATION FOUNDATION

CHINESE RED
中国红

风 筝

Kites

李鹏◎编著

全国百佳图书出版单位
时代出版传媒股份有限公司
黄 山 书 社

图书在版编目(CIP)数据

风筝: 汉英对照 / 李鹏编著. -- 合肥：黄山书社，
2013.6

（中国红）

ISBN 978-7-5461-3599-1

Ⅰ. ①风… Ⅱ. ①李… Ⅲ. ①风筝—介绍—中国—
汉、英 Ⅳ. ①J528.6

中国版本图书馆CIP数据核字(2013)第098061号

风筝
FENG ZHENG

李　鹏　编著

出 版 人：任耕耘

责任编辑：司　雯　　　　　　　　　　特约编辑：包云鸠
责任印制：戚　帅　李　磊　　　　　　装帧设计：商子庄

出版发行：时代出版传媒股份有限公司（http://www.press-mart.com）
　　　　　黄山书社（http://www.hsbook.cn）
　　　　　（合肥市蜀山区翡翠路1118号出版传媒广场7层　邮编：230071）
经　　销：新华书店　　　　　　　　　营销电话：0551-63533762　63533768
印　　刷：安徽联众印刷有限公司　　　电　　话：0551-65661327

开　　本：710×875　1/16　　　　　　印张：9.5　　字数：125千字
版　　次：2013年6月第1版　　2013年6月第1次印刷
书　　号：ISBN 978-7-5461-3599-1　　　　定价：59.00元

风筝是以竹篾等材料扎制而成的一种工艺精湛、制作精巧的手工艺品。风筝不仅是游乐竞技中的玩具，而且具有测距、通信、载人等功能。中国的风筝艺术源远流长，2700多年前春秋时代第一只木鸢的诞生，便揭开了其发展的序幕。英国科学史专家李约瑟博士在《中国科学技术史》中把风筝列为中国向欧洲传播的重大科技发明之一，美国国家博物馆中展示风筝的一块牌子上写着："世界上最早的飞行器是中国的风筝和火箭。"中国的风筝作品精彩纷呈，形成了多个具有浓厚地域特色的风筝流派，而且与绘画、民俗等内容结合在

Kites are beautiful handicrafts works made with bamboo slips. Some are toys, while others have a practical use, ranging, message sending and man carrying. Kite making has a long history in China, possibly beginning with the first wooden glede made by ancient people over 2700 years ago during the Spring and Autumn Period. Dr. Joseph Needham, established British scholar in the history of sciences, listed kite making in his famous book *Science and Civilization in China* as one of the significant events in civilization, an invention later spreading to Europe. A signboard inside the United States National Museum says the following: "Kites and rockets made in China are the earliest aircrafts man ever made in his history."

一起，有着丰富的文化内涵。

　　本书以生动的文字和直观的图片，向海内外读者全面介绍中国风筝的起源、发展历程、分类、制作工艺、流派，以及风筝文化等内容，希望能够引领读者了解中国风筝知识，品鉴风筝艺术的绚烂多姿。

Kite making in China became stylistically diversified to characterize regional culture. By involving painting and local customs, kites carry profound cultural message.

　　By brief introduction and beautiful plates, this booklet makes an endeavor helping peoples of other countries understand kites' origin, development, categories, making technique and styles, as well as the cultural message they carry.

目 录 | Contents

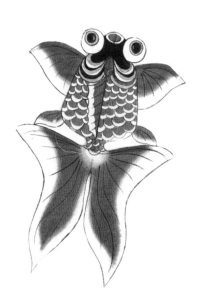

风筝史话
History of Kites

中国风筝的历史源远流长，从春秋时期的第一只木鸢问世起，至今已有两千多年的历史。用于放飞的风筝在古时被称为"纸鸢"、"木鸢"或"鹞"，是人们日常生活中的娱乐玩具之一。然而，古代的风筝并不只是用于游艺玩乐，其功能经历了多次变化，并最终形成了丰富多彩、奇绝精巧的风筝艺术。

The long history of kite making in China began with the first wooden glede made during the Spring and Autumn Period over two thousand years ago. Kites made for flying had different names, "paper glede", "wooden glede" or "snipe". As a toy, they gave people much fun. Their function, however, was not limited to entertainment. Their evolution eventually left us a rich and colorful art form.

> 风筝的起源

　　国内外学者对风筝的起源有多种争议，但大多数人都认为风筝最早源起于中国。英国科学史专家李约瑟博士在《中国科学技术史》中引用了明代王逵《蠡海集》里关于利用风筝测量风力和风向的记述，并认为风筝是中国向欧洲输送的科技发明之一。而英国民俗学家克里·哈特则在《风筝——历史的考察》中总结了中国风筝向世界传输

> The Birth of Kites

Scholars are quite diversified in establishing the birth of kites, but most of them believed it happened in China. In *Science and Civilization in China*, Dr. Joseph Needham, based on the book *Du Hai Ji* authored by a Ming-dynasty person named Wang Kui about the use of kites for measuring the force and direction of wind, ascribed it as an invention by ancient Chinese people but later spreading to Europe. Another British scholar, Clive Hart, went further

● 树木风筝纹瓦当（战国）
此瓦当的右下角有一只简易的风筝，表明在战国时期风筝已经问世。
Eaves Tile with Kite and Tree Design (Warring States Period)
A kite on the lower right corner proves the birth of kite already happened during the Warring States Period.

- 编年体史书《资治通鉴》（书影）

《资治通鉴》共294卷，是司马光历时19年主编而成的一部多卷本编年体史书。其以时间为纲、事件为目，涵盖了从周代到五代共16朝1362年的历史。作为中国第一部编年体通史，其在中国官修史书中占有非常重要的地位。

History as a Mirror in Annalistic Style (photo image)

This 294-volumn colossal book cost Sima Guang 19 years to complete. By following a timeline, it documents all significant events that had happened over the past 1362 years in 16 dynasties put together. This book, as the first history work in annalistic style written with the authorization from ruler, has its notch cut in Chinese history.

的几条路线：一是从中国经朝鲜、日本、马来半岛、大洋洲、新西兰至复活节岛；二是由中国经过缅甸、印度、阿拉伯国家及北非，最终到达地中海沿岸；三是自中国经由蒙古至俄罗斯、东欧、到达欧洲大陆；四是自中国经由丝绸之路到达欧洲，再转至美洲。

中国关于风筝最早的详细记述见于《韩非子·外储说左上》："（墨子）斫木为鹞，三年而成，飞一日而败。"意思是说战国时期的墨子花了三年的时间用木头造出一只木鹞，但只飞了一天就坏了。北宋司马光主编的编年体史书《资治通鉴》里也记载了有关风筝的事迹。南北朝时期（420—

as to work out the routes Chinese kites had taken when going to the rest parts of the world: from China to Korea, further on to Japan, Malaya, Oceania, New Zealand and the Easter Island. The second route, by Clive Harter in his book *Kites: An Historical Survey*, was from China to Burma, India, Arab countries, North Africa and the areas around the Mediterranean. The third one was from China to Mongolia, Russia, Eastern Europe and the rest parts of European continent. The fourth was from China and via the Silk Road, to Europe, and further on to America.

The first document about kites was found in a book, *Philosophical Notes*, by ancient philosopher named Han Feizi. The wooden glede costing Mozi three

墨子

　　墨子是战国时期著名的思想家、教育家、科学家、军事家，墨家学派的创始人。墨学在当时影响很大，与儒家并称"显学"，在春秋战国的百家争鸣中有"非儒即墨"之称。墨子还创立了以几何学、物理学、光学为主要内容的一整套科学理论，并且精通手工技艺，制作出了能够飞行的木鸟（风筝），载重30石（合120斤）、运行迅速又省力的车辆。另外，墨子也熟悉当时的各种兵器、机械和工程建筑的制造技术，其在《墨子》一书中详细介绍和阐述了城市中各种防御设施的构造，弓、弩、刀、剑、矛、盾、斧等攻守器械的制造工艺，以及水道和地道的构筑技术。墨子论及的这些器械和设施，对后世的城市兴建和军事活动有着很大的影响。

Mozi

Famous thinker, educator, scientist and militarist during the Warring States Period, Mozi had a huge influence in his time. The philosophy he established stood shoulder to shoulder with Confucian school, and together with the latter, called *Xian Xue* studies. Being a follower of either Confucian school or Mozi doctrines, people said about everyone. Apart from philosophical beliefs, Mozi initiated studies in geometry, physics and optics. Mozi was also a master handicraftsman, able to make wooden gledes and carts of 60 kilos carrying capacity. Mozi was well-versed in weaponry, mechanics and engineering. In his book titled after him, he detailed the making of different weapons including blades, swords, arrows and bows, as well as the tunneling and water channeling techniques for military purposes. The discoveries and inventions he made had huge influence on later generations' infrastructural and military projects.

● 墨子塑像（图片提供：FOTOE）
Statue of Mozi

589）的侯景作乱时，叛军将梁武帝围困于梁都建邺（今江苏南京）。面对内外围困的形势，一个名叫羊车儿的人建议将梁武帝的诏令藏在纸鸱中，然后随风放飞纸鸱，以向外求援。可见，风筝的产生最早可追溯到春秋战国时期（前770—前221），而其由雏形逐渐演变成熟则在汉代（前206—公元220）至南北朝时期。

在民间，关于风筝的起源也有多种传说，其中流传最广的是飞鸟说、树叶斗笠说和帆船说这三种。飞鸟说与《韩非子》中的记述近

years to make was damaged the first day it was used. Sima Guang, historian during the Northern Song Dynasty, also documented kites in his book *Zi Zhi Tong Jian*, or *History as a Mirror*. When Ruler Liang Wu was besieged in Liang capital Jianye, present-day Nanjing by rebellious army during the Northern and Southern Dynasties (420-589), a man suggested to the ruler sending SOS message by a paper kite to fly in wind for his troops. These documents show the birth of kites did happen in China during the Spring and Autumn Period (770 B.C.-221 B.C.) and their making techniques matured around the Han (206 B.C.-220 A.D.) to Northern and Southern Dynasties.

Common people tell different versions about the birth of kites, the most popular being three: coming from

● 斗笠

斗笠是一种遮阳和避雨的编结帽，是古代江南农村生产生活中必不可少的物品，至今仍然随处可见。斗笠轻盈，能在风力作用下自由飞舞，人们受飘飞的斗笠的启发而产生了制作风筝的想法。

Bamboo Hat

A necessary item in rural life in southern part of China, bamboo hats are able to keep off strong sunshine and rain. They are still popular today. Very light in weight, a bamboo hat is able to fly in wind and because of this, ancient people managed to make kites.

- 树叶风筝

树叶风筝流行于中国南方及沿海地区，将阔叶树木的树叶晾干后直接固定在骨架上，就形成了一个完整的风筝。由于骨架也多就地取材，因而树叶风筝造型古朴。

Tree Leaf Kites

This kind of kite, popular in China's south and coastal areas, is made with dried up leaves of broad-leaved trees pasted on a structure, which is also made with local material. Kites of this kind look very primitive.

似，均是从飞鸟获得启发而制作出可飞行的器物。树叶斗笠说是看到树叶或斗笠在风力作用下飞舞的情形而产生制作风筝的想法，如生活在台湾的高山族和生活在海南的黎族人都用槟榔树的叶子做过风筝。风筝的放飞不仅是为了娱乐，也属于祭祀形式，是人们表达对漫天飞舞的树叶的崇拜的一种形式。帆船说是根据风帆借助风力前行的原理制作并放飞风筝的说法。

bird flying, coming from tree leaves and bamboo hat, and coming from a sail boat. The first one is similar with the writing by Han Feizi, ascribing the birth to a flying bird. The second came from leaves flying in wind. The Gaoshan people in Taiwan and Li people in Hainan had made kites with areca catechu leaves. Flying a kite, to people, was more than for entertainment. It was also a form of worshipping out of the admiration of leaves flying in the sky. The third version possibly came from the sail propelled by wind force.

> 风筝的发展历程

> Evolution of Kites

通过探究风筝的起源，可以看到在风筝的发展历史上其功能有多次变化，除了娱乐，风筝还多应用在军事、测量、通信、祭祀等方面。

从汉代到南北朝时期，风筝主

The evolution of kites shows their use developed, apart from amusement, for military, measuring, communication and worshipping purposes.

Their military use happened during the Han Dynasty and the Southern and Northern Dynasties that followed. By

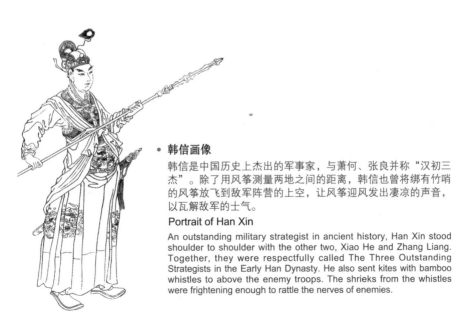

● **韩信画像**

韩信是中国历史上杰出的军事家，与萧何、张良并称"汉初三杰"。除了用风筝测量两地之间的距离，韩信也曾将绑有竹哨的风筝放飞到敌军阵营的上空，让风筝迎风发出凄凉的声音，以瓦解敌军的士气。

Portrait of Han Xin

An outstanding military strategist in ancient history, Han Xin stood shoulder to shoulder with the other two, Xiao He and Zhang Liang. Together, they were respectfully called The Three Outstanding Strategists in the Early Han Dynasty. He also sent kites with bamboo whistles to above the enemy troops. The shrieks from the whistles were frightening enough to rattle the nerves of enemies.

● **瓷壁画《金凤台》**（图片提供：FOTOE）
此图为绘在瓷砖上的壁画，展现了邺城三台之中的铜雀台和金凤台，其中左面即为文宣帝让囚犯乘风筝向下飞的金凤台。

Golden Phoenix Terrace, Ceramic Painting
It pictures two of the three famous terraces in Yecheng: Bronze Sparrow and Golden Phoenix. The left one was the Golden Phoenix, the terrace from which prisoners were instructed to glide down on kites.

要作军事之用。如在宋代高承的《事物纪原》中，记载了汉代大将军韩信曾将风筝放飞到空中，根据风筝线的长度来测量两地之间距离的事情。史书《北史》中也记载了南北朝时期北齐的文宣帝曾下令让囚犯乘风筝从邺城的金凤台上向下飞行，能够飞出城的便赦免其死罪，而一个名叫黄头的人就成功地

Records of Things, a book by Han-dynasty Gao Cheng, army general Han Xin once measured the distance from spot A to B by sending a kite into sky. Ruler Wenxuan of the Beiqi Regime, by Northern History, had prisoners glide down on a kite from a high terrace out of the town. Anyone who succeeded in doing so was pardoned from death penalty. The lucky one was named Huang

飘到了城外。金凤台的遗址在今河北临漳县城西，残台高12米。当时的风筝能载着人飞行相当长的距离，可见其形制、体积之大和扎制、放飞技术的成熟。这也间接体现出了那时的人们对风能的认识和利用均具有一定的水平。

唐代（618—907）是中国历史上国力最强盛的朝代之一，物质上的丰富促进了节庆民俗娱乐的增多。而此时风筝的娱乐功能也开始突显。纸的应用是风筝得以在民间普及的关键，风筝裱糊所用的材质由绢改为纸，使风筝的制作成本降低，重量减轻。这样，风筝逐渐就成为了市井中较为普遍的娱乐用品。与此同时，风筝的类型也开始增多，出现了造型风筝和可发声的风筝。造型风筝多以素纸装饰，当

Tou, who landed successfully outside the town. That terrace was named Jinfeng, meaning golden phoenix, whose relics are still there west to the Linzhang County seat of Hebei Province. The remaining part is still 12 meters tall. Gliding down from it on a kite shows the kite making techniques, as well as structuring and flying, was matured, able to handle a big size to fly over a long distance from a perilous height. People then must have gained much knowledge about wind force.

As one of the most powerful dynasties in Chinese history, Tang (618-907) had more holidays and entertaining forms out of abundant supplies than any dynasty before or after. Amusement with kites was more emphasized. Replacement of silk by paper for kite making considerable cut the cost and weight,

• **风筝制作材料中的宣纸**
用于制作风筝的纸张要求纤维长、韧性好、密度大、易上色和延展性低，这包括绵纸、宣纸、高丽纸等手工纸，以及拷贝纸、油封纸、绝缘纸等机制纸。

Xuan Paper Used for Kite Making

The paper for kite making must have longer fibers, tenacious and dense in texture, easy to pick up colors and be plastic. Paper able to meet these demands includes *Xuan* paper, tissue and Korean paper made by hand. Copy paper, oil seal paper and insulation paper made by machines also work.

• 风筝上的声响装置
装有哨子的风筝在放飞后借助风力的作用，能发出幽远的声音。
The Sound Device for Kites
Kites with whistles gave a simple but long-drawn sound in wind.

时人们对风筝图案的绘画要求并不多。可发声的风筝上多装置有弓弦，放飞时气流吹动弓弦发出如筝的声音，这也是风筝名称的由来。

enabling more varieties to happen. Kites became popular toys in society. Some kites emphasized on looks, while others, on the sound they made. People then, however, were less emphatic on the

唐诗中的风筝
Tang Poem About Flying Kites

在唐诗中有大量对当时放飞风筝的描写,如元稹的《有鸟》:

> 有鸟有鸟群纸鸢,因风假势童子牵。
>
> 去地渐高人眼乱,世人为尔羽毛全。
>
> 风吹绳断童子走,余势尚存犹在天。
>
> 愁尔一朝还到地,落在深泥谁复怜。

Many Tang poems have kites as subject matter, among them, *You Niao*, or *Bird* by Yuan Zhen, was probably the most chanted:

● 放风筝图(图片提供:FOTOE)
Picture of *Sending a Kite to Fly*

A kite bird is flying in the air,

The end of its thread is held in a boy's hand.

It's flying over places high and low,

And people take it as a fully fledged bird.

All of a sudden, the thread is cut,

But the kite keeps flying.

Somewhere, it will land,

To be pitied by someone unknown.

　　诗中所描述的纸鸢与今天的风筝在形制与放飞技术上基本相同，从纸鸢的名称则可看出当时风筝的裱糊材质以纸质为主。

These paper birds had a similar way sent to fly with what people do today. Their name suggested the popular material of paper mounted on a structure.

还有记载，五代（907—960）时的李邺曾将竹笛安装在风筝上，放飞时气流通过竹笛发出的声音比弓弦的声音更加悦耳。声响风筝的出现表明当时人们对于气流有了很高程度的认识与利用。

宋代（960—1279）是中国风筝的繁荣发展阶段。宋代经济文化发达，民间手工业兴起，传统的节日风俗也得到朝廷的大力提倡，这些都促进了风筝的发展和娱乐功能

graphic image that appeared on kites, so many had plain paper without drawings. Sound device was placed on the back of a kite. The air flow was like a hand plucking at a string, giving a musical sound as if from an instrument. This was the reason why kite in Chinese was called *feng zheng*, meaning "a wind musical instrument". Li Ye of the Five Dynasties (907-960) once mounted a bamboo flute on a kite for a more musical sound than a string being plucked. Sound kites show people then had knowledge about aero-

的进一步深化。在北宋著名画家张择端所绘的城市风俗画《清明上河图》中可以看到描绘幼儿郊外放风筝的场景。宋代工明清所著的《挥麈录》中则记载了北宋皇帝宋徽宗在即位之初，曾于闲暇时放纸鸢为戏。

权贵及文人阶层的参与，使得风筝在制作技艺和文化传承上更加丰富多彩。放风筝成为当时民间的重要游艺活动，是孩童和成年人共

dynamics.

Kite making experienced fast progress during the Song Dynasty (960-1279), a period in Chinese history with highly developed culture and handicraft. Traditional festivals were much valued by the government. All these promoted the development of kite making and their entertaining side. Flying kite was found in the famous painting by Zhang Zeduan, a Song-dynasty painter, *Upper River During Qingming Festival*, which

● **中国画《清明上河图》【局部】张择端（北宋）**

《清明上河图》是中国十大传世名画之一，作品以长卷形式，采用散点透视的构图法，生动地记录了12世纪时中国城市生活的风貌，展现了宋代的人文风俗及建筑特色。此图为局部图，描绘了幼儿在郊外放风筝的画面。

Upper River During Qingming Festival [part], Traditional Chinese Painting by Zhang Zeduan (Northern Song Dynasty)

As one of the top ten paintings in Chinese ancient history, this painting was a long roll done by cavalier perspective. It depicts urban life during the 12th century in China, showing the customs and buildings then. This part is a detail showing a child flying a kite on a suburb.

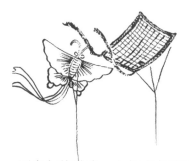

同参与的游戏，人们或者将脸谱制成风筝放飞到空中以愉悦心情，或者把诗、画绘到风筝上以陶冶情操，或者举行形式多样的风筝竞技比赛。而随着风筝游艺活动的频繁，宋代的风筝品种不断增多、玩法不断翻新，还出现了专门制作风筝和被称为"赶趁人"的专门放飞

illustrated, apart from other scenes, a young boy did it for fun on a suburb. By Wang Mingqing's book, *Anecdotes of the Time*, during the early years of Emperor Huizong of the Northern Song Dynasty in the throne, he flew kites in spare time.

The interest from the rich and powerful boosted kite making, making it more diversified in style and looks. Flying kite became part of festivity, particularly to children, who did it with adults. Kites made then had human faces, a painting or a poem on them and flying such a kite was indeed a very enjoyable

• 儿童放风筝图
Picture of *Children Flying Kites*

风筝的人。

宋代周密所著的《武林旧事》把临安（今杭州）经营风筝的人放在"小经济"专栏，更将放风筝与书会、戏狮、吞刀、舞巨兽等55种杂技放在一起，以表明放风筝"此虽小技，亦有专门"。另外，此书还详细记述了风筝艺人周三、吕扁头的事迹，以及宋代风筝放飞时的场景和斗风筝的风俗。

元代（1279—1368），风筝的传播范围扩大至西南少数民族地区，史料中有风筝在当时的战争中充当通信工具的记载。虽然元代统

activity. Competitions were held, in which participants competed one another in skills. More varieties came into being and the way to fly was diversified.

Old Incidents in Wulin, a book by Zhou Mi, a Song-dynasty writer, listed kite makers in this trade together with people in others trades like book deal, lion dance, swallowing knives and other acrobatic performance total 55 to show the acknowledgement this trade possessed: small as it was, it was equal with others. Zhou Mi even detailed some kite making or flying masters like Zhou San and Lv Biantou and the spectacular scenes of flying kites during the Song Dynasty. Some were able to do a "kite fight" in the sky.

Flying kites during the Yuan Dynasty (1279-1368) was also found in remote areas of southwest of China lived in by ethnic minority groups. Kites used as means of sending message in a battle

• 版画《绯衣梦》
此为书生放风筝时与未婚妻巧遇的场景。其未婚妻因不舍与书生之间的情谊，决定赠送钱财给书生以作为迎娶自己的聘礼。
Dream of Red Dress, Wood-block Print
This is the part when the young scholar met his fiancée. The latter helps the former with betrothal money for the marriage.

治者推行禁铁的政策，十户人家共用一把菜刀，使风筝的发展因缺少制造工具而受到极大的限制，但风筝在民间依然盛行。在元代剧作家关汉卿所著的剧本《绯衣梦》中，便讲述了一个贫穷书生在遭遇有钱岳父的退婚后，因放风筝的际遇最终与未婚妻结成夫妻的故事。从剧中人物之间的对话可见当时放风筝的热闹情形。

到了明代（1368—1644），风筝的发展出现了北禁南盛之势。明初，由于统治者害怕风筝被用做谋反的工具，明政府禁止在京都（今北京）放风筝，因而北方地区放风筝的习俗受到了一定的影响。但

were recorded in history books. Yuan government placed a very tight control on iron use; it allowed ten households possessing just one cutting knife. Due to the lack of necessary tools kite making suffered a very slow progress. But flying kite was still popular in society. *Dream of Red Dress*, a play script by Yuan-dynasty writer Guan Hanqing, tells a romance that happened between two young people. The poor young scholar was forced to give up engagement with a young lady from a rich family by his future father-in-law, but an experience of flying kite eventually made the two into a marriage bond. The dialogues in the play show how popular flying kite was then.

By the Ming Dynasty (1368-1644), kite making and flying was banned in the north, particularly around Beijing, because the Ming government was fearful

在南方，清明节放风筝是一项不可缺少的活动，扫墓结束后人们会在坟前放起风筝。风筝不仅在白天放飞，夜间也放。在风筝上或拉线上挂上一串串彩色小灯笼，在夜空中闪闪发光，这被人们看做是能够带来好运的"神灯"。此时，风筝成为画家和诗人常用的创作题材。如明代著名诗人、书画家徐渭留下数十首咏风筝的题画诗，其中的"柳

this activity might serve as an instrument for rebels to pass message. In the south, flying kite was still allowed, particularly during the Qingming Festival, After a memorial ceremony held before the burial ground people would fly kites, even at night. Strings of small lanterns attached to the kite and the thread lit up the evening sky. This was taken as a sign of good luck. Kites made a frequent subject matter for artists and writers. Xu

● 中国画《山水花卉人物图册》【局部】 徐渭（明）
该图册共十八页，其中画有十五页，内容为写意山水、写生花卉、婴戏图、对弈图等。此图是其中之一，为一儿童正在放风筝，反映了明代放风筝的习俗。

Landscape, Flowers and People, Illustrated Book [part] by Xu Wei (Ming Dynasty)

15 of the 18 pages are given to pictures, showing landscape, flowers, baby at play, people playing chess. One of them has a child flying kite to show this popular practice during the Ming Dynasty.

● **青花婴戏罐（明）**

此青花瓷器的图案为几个儿童放风筝，位于中间位置的儿童在看到风筝飞起来后，高兴得手舞足蹈。

Blue-and-white Porcelain Pot with Babies at Play (Ming Dynasty)

Several children are seen flying kites. The one in the center is wild with excitement when the kite is up.

● **天津杨柳青年画《童戏风筝》** （图片提供：FOTOE）

杨柳青年画约产生于明代崇祯年间(1628—1643)，是中国著名的民间木版年画，与苏州桃花坞年画并称为"南桃北柳"。此年画上的图案为几个儿童在河岸边放风筝，虽然风筝的形制简单，但表明了放风筝在儿童的娱乐活动中占有重要地位。

Children Flying Kites, New Year Painting from Yangliuqing, Tianjin

Famous Yangliuqing style New Year painting first appeared during the Chongzhen Reign of the Ming Dynasty (1628-1643) to compete with the southern Taohuawu style in Suzhou. In this painting, several children are seen flying kites by a river. Simple as these kites were, they made an important part in children's life then.

清明节

　　清明节是中国民间传统节日，一般是在公历4月5日前后。清明节起源于中国古代帝王将相的"墓祭"之礼，后来民间也效仿着在此日祭祖扫墓，并历代沿袭，成为中华民族的一种固定的风俗节日。清明节的习俗丰富多彩，不仅讲究禁火、扫墓，还有踏青、荡秋千、蹴鞠、打马球、插柳、放风筝等一系列体育活动。因此，这个节日中既有祭扫坟墓的悲伤，又有踏青游玩的欢快，是一个富有特色的节日。

The Qingming Festival

The traditional Qingming Festival (Clear and Bright Festival) often falls around April 5. It came from the memorial services rulers did in ancient China. After the practice spread to lower society, it became traditional to mourn the dead. This festival used to have many activities, but fire was not allowed on this day. Apart from a memorial service held before a tomb, people did outing in the country, playing on a swing, kicking a ball, an ancient form of polo, or planting willows and flying kites. So this festival was both happy and sad, but a very good excuse for taking a day off to walk in fields.

● 宋词画谱《春游》中的踏青场景
Spring Outing, a Scene Described in a Verse from the Song Dynasty

条搓线絮搓棉，搓够千寻放纸鸢"等诗句形象地反映了明代民间放风筝的情景。

清代（1644—1911）是风筝发展史上的鼎盛时期。工商业的迅速发展和民俗活动的增多使这一时期的风筝形成多种流派，风筝的风格化和艺术化特征更加明显。无论在宫廷还是在民间，放风筝已经成为人们春季或秋季外出游玩的一项重要活动和节日民俗中不可缺少的部分。

放风筝的内容也被写入文学作品中。如李渔所著的《风筝误》就

Wei, famous poet of the Ming Dynasty, composed dozens of poems about kites. Some are still chanted today.

Kite making peaked during the Qing Dynasty (1644-1911). Due to the fast progress of industry and commerce, and with more folklore activities than any period of history before, kites exhibited more styles and became more artistic. For both royal families and commoners, flying kite was part of the activities people did when doing an outing, or celebrating a festival.

Many literary works have it as a part. *Mistake out of Flying Kite* by Li Yu tells how a marriage happens: a young

• 版画《风筝误》中放风筝的场景
在此图的右下角，庭院中的的女子正在将一只拖着长尾巴的风筝放飞。

Scene from the Story *Mistake out of Flying Kite*, Wood-block Print
On the lower right corner, a young lady in courtyard is flying a kite with a long tail.

● 《北京民间风俗百图》中放风筝的场景

此图展现的是一个清代男子放风筝的场景，男子头戴瓜皮帽，身穿蓝色长袍、外罩黑色对襟马褂，左手握着缠绕风筝线的轴轮，右手则抓着系有蝴蝶风筝的长线。

Scenes of Flying Kites from *Folk Customs in Beijing*

This picture shows a man during the Qing Dynasty flying a kite. In a traditional style skullcap, a blue robe under a mandarin vest, he was holding a thread wheeler in one hand and the thread in the other. At the end of the thread was a butterfly kite.

是以风筝作为缘起，说的是才子韩生在风筝上题诗，风筝放飞后由于提线折断而被一个女子捡到，那女子也在风筝上题了诗句，然后又将风筝重新放飞，由此而引发了一段姻缘的故事。另外，人们也开始对风筝工艺进行研究和探索。如古典名著《红楼梦》的作者曹雪芹，在对中国风筝的发展历史、扎制工艺

scholar inscribed on his kite before he flew it. The thread was snapped and the kite was found by a young lady, who inscribed a poem on the kite before she sent it back to the sky. Craftsmen, even men of letters, made efforts to improve the making techniques. A fine example was Cao Xueqin, author of *Dream of Red Mansion*, who did much research into the history, varieties and making techniques

和种类等做了大量考研的基础上，写出了中国第一部关于风筝艺术的专著《南鹞北鸢考工志》。此后，风筝的分类更加细化，特技风筝的出现增加了人们放飞风筝时的乐趣。风筝的材质也更加多样化，特别是上层社会对风筝的需求，促进了风筝向精致化的方向发展。

of kites. Based on his research, he wrote a monograph *Kite Making in the South and North.* Beginning from his time, kite categories became more detailed, which gave more fun to people when flew them. The materials for kite making became diversified. Demand from upper class was huge for elaborately made kites.

● **清代的风筝铺**

此图出自《营业写真》，图中为售卖各类风筝的风筝铺。风筝铺里的卖家正在给顾客展示蜻蜓风筝。

Kite Shop in the Qing Dynasty

This picture from *Commercial Business* illustrates a shop selling varieties of kites. The shop assistant is busy with customers, showing a dragonfly kite to one of them.

- **双葫芦风筝（清）**
  此双葫芦风筝为上下结构，上面为葫芦叶，下面
  是两个并排的红色葫芦，葫芦上装饰寿字纹，寓
  意长寿。

  Twin-gourd Kite (Qing Dynasty)
  This kite has two parts, the upper part being leaves
  and the lower part two gourds in red color, inscribed
  on their bodies are characters of "longevity".

曹雪芹与《红楼梦》中的风筝

　　《红楼梦》是曹雪芹写的长篇章回体小说，为中国古代四大名著之一。此书以
贾宝玉、林黛玉的爱情悲剧为主要线索，着重描写了贾家由盛到衰的过程，全面展
现了古代社会的人情世态。书中内容包罗万象，在中国古代社会制度、民间风俗、
古代建筑、诗词曲赋、金石收藏等各领域皆有不可替代的研究价值，被誉为"中国
封建社会的百科全书"。

　　在《红楼梦》中，熟悉风筝制作与放飞技巧的曹雪芹在展现大观园中的生活
时，也曾多次描写了风筝这一中国传统的游艺玩具。如《红楼梦》第七十回所描述
的放风筝情景中就涉及了多种式样的风筝，包括蝴蝶风筝、美人风筝、凤凰风筝、
大鱼风筝、螃蟹风筝、红蝙蝠风筝、大雁风筝、喜字风筝等。此处出现的风筝品种
之多，是之前的文学作品所不能企及的。曹雪芹借助风筝这一工艺品，不仅写出了
大观园内青年男女的无忧无虑，更通过艺术化的手法，以风筝隐喻人物的性格和命
运，如探春扎的凤凰风筝恰是其未来当王妃的喻示。

The Kites Described in *Dream of Red Mansion* by Cao Xueqin

Dream of Red Mansion is one of the four classic novels in Chinese literary history, telling how the super-rich Jia family goes down to poverty. The story centralizes around the romance between Jia Baoyu and Lin Daiyu. It is a picture of the then human relationship, touching almost every aspect in society, political system, folk customs, classical style buildings, literary writings and collection of antiques. This novel is regarded as an encyclopedia about Chinese feudalistic society.

Familiar with the making and flying techniques of kites, Cao Xueqin detailed in the novel about kites, this age-old traditional toy. In chapter 70, he wrote about flying different kinds of kites, more than any book had ever described. Through kites, Cao Xueqin depicts a carefree life of young people in the family, making kites a metaphor for the fate of each. For instance, the golden phoenix kite Tanchun made was a hint for her later development to be a royal concubine.

• 手持芭蕉扇的美人风筝
Kite with a Beauty Holding a Palm-leaf Fan

民国时期（1912—1949），由于资本主义经济的影响，风筝的制作日益市场化。在山东潍坊、北京、天津、江苏南通等地，制作和销售风筝成为一种家庭副业。同时，专业的制作人员越来越多，出现了以潍坊唐家风筝铺为代表的十多家专业风筝铺。

各地画家也广泛地参与到风筝

During the Republican years, due to the influence from Capitalism, kite making was highly commercial and in Weifang of Shandong Province, Beijing, Tianjin and Nantong of Jiangsu Province family business of kite making appeared. More and more people entered this trade, but the most famous were ten shops, among them, the one owned by the Tang family in Weifang being the most

- 泥塑《卖风筝》
此泥塑表现的是老北京街边艺人卖风筝的场景。一个带着孩子的男子正在试着放飞风筝，风筝艺人则在给男子展示着另外一只精美的瘦沙燕风筝。

Clay Sculpture, *Selling Kites*

A man and his child are trying to fly a kite, while the seller was showing him a more impressive one, an elaborately made thin swallow kite.

● **长尾奥运风筝**
此风筝是以2008年北京奥运会为题材的大型风筝，在风筝的绿色长尾巴上写着红色的奥运口号"同一个世界，同一个梦想。"
Long-tail Kite for 2008 Olympics
This kite was made for the 2008 Beijing Olympic Games, with "one world, one dream" inscribed in red on its green tail.

的绘制中，形成了风筝图案的文人画风与民间画风并存的局面。由风筝艺人扎制和画家绘图的高档风筝得到人们的极大喜爱，成为一种挂在墙壁上的艺术品，而不再仅仅用来放飞、娱乐。

这时，风筝也开始走向世界。

representative.

Artists were involved. Scholar's painting kites customer-tailored appeared to exist side by side with traditional patterns. Elaborately made and painted kites were much sought after in market. Apart from flying, they became a decorative item on walls.

1915年，中国风筝第一次参加巴拿马万国博览会，北京风筝艺人哈长英、天津风筝艺人魏元泰制作的风筝分别获得金牌和银牌奖。

新中国成立后，风筝比赛作为一种体育活动活跃于各地区，民间风筝向高层次和多功能方向进一步发展。

Kites went out of China to abroad. In 1915, kites from China, for the first time, were seen on the Panama World Expo and the ones made by Ha Changying from Beijing and Wei Yuantai from Tianjin won a gold and silver prize.

After the founding of PRC, kite flying became a competitive sport and kite making showed improved techniques for more functions.

- 奥运福娃风筝中的"福娃晶晶"、"福娃欢欢"
  福娃是2008年在北京举行的第29届奥运会的吉祥物，五个福娃分别叫"贝贝"、"晶晶"、"欢欢"、"迎迎"、"妮妮"，各取它们名字中的一个字即组成了谐音"北京欢迎你"。

"Jingjing" and "Huanhuan", Kites Made for Beijing 2008 Olympics
The five kites were made for the 2008 Olympic Games, successively named "Beibei", "Jingjing", "Huanhuan", "Yingying" and"Nini". One character from their names, when put together, makes "Welcome to Beijing".

中国风筝比赛中的相关规则

1988年，中国国家体委把风筝列为正式的体育比赛项目。1990年，国家体委颁发了《风筝竞赛规则》。此规则共分为五章，包括比赛通则、风筝的分类标准、评分细则、犯规与失败的评判标准和比赛用的场地、器材标准。其中，一些关于风筝比赛的常规性条例，表明了风筝作为一项比赛具有其特有的属性。如风筝的放飞只能手工操作，不能借助于电动和遥控装置等器材；比赛中不能运用收放线故意缠绕其他参赛者的风筝；风筝的工艺评分完成后，参赛者不能替换和转借风筝，也不能增减风筝的装饰品；三次没有顺利放飞风筝即意味着比赛失败。

The Rules for Kite Flying Competition in China

Kite flying was listed by the government as a competitive sport in 1988 with detailed rules about events, categories, evaluation of performance, foul, failure, the ground to hold a match and equipment needed. Rules specified that kite flying was only to be done by hand, not to be motor-driven or by remote control. No foul is allowed like using a thread to hook other kites when winding and releasing. No kite in the competition was allowed to be replaced or borrowed, nor to add or reduce ornamental objects on it. Failing to be released for three times, the kite was out.

• 风筝比赛现场（图片提供：微图）
Competition Ground

风筝文化
Kite Culture

　　放风筝不仅是一种游戏，而且还与民众祈福、岁时节令活动等有着密切的联系。人们将风筝制作与文化艺术、民俗等相融合，形成了丰富多彩的"风筝文化"，反映了人们对美好生活的向往和追求。
Flying kite is more than a game; it is closely related to people's wish for happiness. By combining artistic elements and customs, makers make kites as a symbol for good wishes and a happy life.

> 风筝与吉祥文化

　　风筝作为一种民间手工艺品，不仅制作精美，而且被赋予了丰富的吉祥寓意。风筝艺人和文人画师通过风筝图案的绘制，表达了人们希望幸福、长寿、喜庆、吉祥与的信仰与愿望。通过放飞风筝，人们希望飞在高处的风筝将愿望带至空中。风筝飞得越高，则表明愿望越容易实现。

> Kites and the Culture of Auspiciousness

As a beautifully made handicraft work, kites are carriers of hope for auspiciousness. Makers and painters, working together, have turned this handicraft work the carrier of good hopes. By flying it, people wish it to carry their hope into the sky. The longer and higher the kite flies, people believe, the more likely their hopes to realize.

Seeking happiness is a common

● 拍子风筝《红章鱼》 唐琦民制
章鱼春天产子，且数量众多。石榴多籽，象征子孙满堂。以章鱼为外形，绘以石榴图案，寓意子孙众多。

Flat Kite *Red Octopus*, Made by Tang Qimin

Octopus gives many eggs in the season of spring, while pomegranate has many seeds. Both mean many sons and grandsons, so painters draw pomegranate in octopus shape to show prosperous posterity.

• 沙燕风筝上的蝙蝠与仙桃图案
象征福气的蝙蝠与寓意长寿的仙桃组合，表示幸福长寿。
The Bat and Peach Painted on Swallow Kites
Bats and peaches, together suggest happiness and longevity.

求福是人们追求幸福的共同心理。风筝上常见的蝙蝠、神仙、葫芦、鲤鱼等图案因为谐音或自身的构造特点，被人们认为是幸福的象征。如蝙蝠因与"遍福"、"遍富"谐音而成为象征福的吉祥图案，较多地出现在北京沙燕等传统风筝上面，像福燕风筝的整个硬翅上就画满了经过美化的蝙蝠。葫芦是中国最原始的吉祥物之一，因谐音"福禄"而象征着和谐美满；另外，由于葫芦多籽而又有多子多福的寓意。以葫芦为图案的风筝比比皆是，在各地都很流行。另外，

psychology. Images appearing on kites like carp, bats, immortals, gourd, because of their homophones in Chinese with the characters to show a kind of good luck, are often seen. Bats are a favored image on swallow kites made in Beijing because bats, in Chinese, are the homophone for "happiness". Swallow kites often carry them on their wings. Gourds are the earliest symbol for happiness in history because their name is the homophone for happiness and officialdom, also because of many seeds they have, taken as a symbol for "many sons". Gourd patterns are very popular. Also, patterns for "happiness and longevity" and "happiness

"福寿双全"、"福在眼前"等风筝也都表达了人们希望通过风筝求福的愿望。

健康长寿在古今之人的心目中都占有重要的地位，风筝上寄寓和祝颂长寿的图案很多，包括万古长青的松柏、寿命能达千年的仙鹤、色彩缤纷的寿带鸟，以及传说中食之可长命百岁的仙草灵芝和能够使人长生不老的西王母仙桃等。除了间接表达长寿寓意的图画纹饰，直接展示长寿的"寿"字的字形图案

comes to the door" are popular.

People hope to maintain healthy and get longevity. Many patterns are for this hope including pine and cypress trees, cranes believed to live for a thousand years, colorful birds of long life span, and magic herbs and peaches able to bring immortality. Apart from these images, shapes for the character of "longevity" in Chinese language are seen in variations, as many as over three hundred. Some images take in the Buddhist symbol " 卍 "to show a hope for brightness,

● 风筝《麻姑献寿》

在民间传说中，麻姑是位神仙，常用桃子接济一些贫困饥饿的老年人。这些老年人吃了桃子之后便觉得神清气爽。于是，人们将此称为"麻姑献寿"。

Kite of *Lady Magu on Birthday Party*

In legend, Magu is a goddess who often helps aged people in need with the peaches she has brought along. After taking the peaches given, these aged people are back to health. So Mugu with her peaches is a popular pattern for kites.

• 硬翅风筝《牡丹花蝶》 哈亦琦制

在中国传统文化中，花中之王的牡丹花象征富贵。蝴蝶形态翩翩、成对嬉戏，故在民间多寓意婚姻美满；蝴蝶的"蝶"还与"耋"字谐音，"耋"指七八十岁的老人，因此蝴蝶又有长寿的含义。蝴蝶、牡丹相结合，寓意富贵长寿。

Hard-wing Kite *Peony and Butterfly*, Made by Ha Yiqi

Peony, taken as the king of flowers, and butterfly able to dance in pair, are taken as the symbol of happy marriage. One word in the Chinese name for butterflies also means "seventy or eighty-year-old man". So butterfly and peony often painted together on kites to mean happy life and longevity.

就达三百多种，变化极为丰富。另外，风筝的图案中还有源于佛教的"卍"字纹样，意为坚固，象征光明有轮回不绝和多至上万的意思。

喜庆表达了人们愉快的心情和热闹的场面，风筝上与此有关的图案包括双喜字、喜鹊、百蝶、百鸟、百花等图案。双喜字由两个并列对称的"喜"字组成，如男女并肩携手而立，象征家庭融洽与美满。风筝中的双喜字除了单独成

eternity and endlessness.

Patterns of happiness and good fortune often appear on kites. They include "double happiness", "magpie", "hundred butterflies or birds" and "hundred flowers". "Double happiness" is made with two characters of happiness standing together, like a man holding a woman's hand to show a happy matrimonial life. This image may appear alone on a kite, or with another pattern to highlight happiness, longevity and

- 硬翅风筝《双喜》 哈亦琦制

  双喜寓意幸福美满，是中国婚礼中必不可少的喜庆元素。以文字"喜"为风筝的基本结构，装饰以花卉，既有吉庆的寓意，又显示出高洁清雅的风貌。

  Hard-wing Kite *Double Happiness*, Made by Ha Yiqi

  "Double happiness" is never missing in a Chinese wedding. On kites, the character is painted with flowers to show happiness, festivity and elegance.

- 风筝《六合蛙鸣》 孔令民制

  六合指东、西、南、北四个方向及上方天、下方地。此风筝上的六只青蛙代表六个方位，其居于寓意高洁的莲叶之上鸣叫，意在赞颂生活和谐美好。

  Kite *Croaking Frogs in Six Directions*, Made by Kong Lingmin

  The six directions mean north, south, east, west, heaven and earth, each being represented by a frog resting on a lotus leaf in this drawing. Their croaking is a song of happy life.

图，还与其他图案结合在一起，组成喜上眉梢、双喜登眉、喜庆有余、福禄寿喜等类别的喜庆风筝。喜鹊在中国自古就是喜事的征兆，特别是牛郎织女鹊桥仙会图在风筝图案中尤为盛行。百蝶、百鸟、百花等气氛热烈、画面壮观的喜庆图案，实际上就是人们通过众多动植物的欣欣向荣来表达安定、愉悦的心情。

与吉祥如意有关的风筝图案很多，较为常见的有龙、凤、麒麟、龟等传说中的祥禽瑞兽和如意等器

officialdom to be achieved. The magpie is a harbinger of good news in Chinese culture, often seen in the story of Niulang and Zhinv. The hero and the heroine are often seen meeting on a heaven bridge built by magpies. This pattern is much favored by kite makers. Butterflies, birds and flowers in full bloom are combined to suggest prosperity and happiness.

There are more auspicious patterns on kites: dragon, phoenix, Qilin and turtle, also legendary animals. The dragon is taken as the king of animals with scales, phoenix, the queen of birds while Qilin (Kylin), king of animals on

● **硬拍子风筝《金蟾》 中国美术馆藏**
金蟾为蟾蜍的神化。在中国的神话传说中，蟾蜍常作为伴在神话人物身边的动物出现，如月宫中的金蟾、刘海身边的三足金蟾等。因此，金蟾在中国传统文化中有招财的吉祥寓意。

Golden Toad, Flat and Hard-wing Kite in the Collection of National Art Museum of China

Golden toad is an immortal in Chinese mythology often seen next to a immortal figure like the one in the moon and the three-feet one next to Liu Hai. In traditional culture, golden toad has a special possession symbolizing for good fortune.

- 风筝《凤凰》

  凤凰是具有灵性的神禽，传说中生性高洁，出现即预示吉祥。此风筝上的凤凰细眼、羽翎长，体现出凤凰的优雅高洁。

  Kite *Phoenix*

  A magic bird, phoenix is a symbol for auspiciousness. The one on this pattern has narrow but long eyes and long feathers, suggesting the wisdom and noble manner it possesses.

- 风筝《麒麟送子》

  麒麟送子是中国民间传统的吉祥装饰图案之一，意指圣明之世的神兽麒麟送来的童子，长大以后一定是经世良材、辅国贤臣。

  Kite *Qilin Delivering Baby*

  This is also a popular pattern, showing a baby delivered by immortal Qilin will grow into a prominent man of the state.

物。其中，龙为百鳞之长、凤为百禽之长、麒麟为百兽之长、龟为百介之长，龙、凤、麒麟、龟合称为"四灵"，在中国人的观念中一直寓意祥和安定，因而成为风筝上的常见图案。它们或单独出现在风筝中，或者互相组合出现，或者与其他动物结合，种类多样，有"龙凤呈祥"风筝、"二龙戏珠"风筝等。如意是具有中国传统特色的吉祥器物，尤其是在清代时期的贵族间极为盛行，皇宫内的宝座旁、寝殿中均摆有如意，以示吉祥、顺心。另外，如意的外形美观雅致，因而成为风

land and turtle, the king of animals in water. Together, they make the idea of "four spirits", symbol of peaceful life and auspiciousness of other kinds. They may appear alone on a kite, or together with other images. Popular ones are "two dragons playing with a pearl", and "dragon and phoenix in heavenly harmony". Apart from these images, a common decorative item in life, *Ruyi*,

• 人们放飞具有吉祥寓意的龙头蜈蚣风筝（图片提供：FOTOE）

Flying the Dragon-headed Centipede Kite with Hope for Auspiciousness

筝中不可或缺的吉祥图案。

人们将风筝放得高而远，然后把风筝线割断让风筝随风飘去，寓意一年来的积郁之气被彻底放了出去，在新的一年里可以幸福安康。中国的文学作品中有许多关于放风筝祛灾的描述，如中国四大名著之一的《红楼梦》第七十回中就专门描写了放风筝祛灾的故事。说的是一个大蝴蝶风筝飘落到大观园的竹梢上，丫环赶紧让人把风筝送出去的过程。

often found by the throne or an emperor's bed, is also a popular pattern to be seen on kites.

Flying kite is also for getting rid of a bad luck, people believe. After the kite flies into sky, the flier may cut the thread and let the kite go, meaning "getting rid of bad luck in that year and have a better year in the next." Many literary works have this belie as a part, like *Dream of Red Mansion*. In chapter 70 servant girls were sent to remove a kite accidently landed in a tree inside the garden.

人们让风筝在天空中自由飘荡以祛灾

（图片提供：微图）

Let Kite Fly Free and High in the Air, an Act Supposedly to Get Rid of Bad Luck.

> 风筝与民俗文化

放风筝习俗的普及，不仅丰富了人们的文化娱乐生活，而且也在发展中与各地的民俗事项互相影响与结合，形成了别具一格的风筝民俗文化。

在中国的大部分地区，风筝主要在春、秋两季放飞，这主要与风力以及中国传统的农耕时节有关。春、秋两季风向平稳，风速适中，适合室外的放风筝活动。而夏天炎热、雷雨多，冬日寒冷、风力猛烈、风向多变，均不是放风筝的良好季节。另外，作为传统农业大国的中国，游艺竞技活动多和农业的时令有关，一般在农闲时进行。在农村地区，自农历十月份到第二年的四月份为农闲季节，农民主要进行农田管理、农用机具整理修补，闲暇时间较多，会做手工艺的农民

> Kites and Folk Culture

Flying kite, while entertaining people, makes another dimension for local custom to progress. Kite as a folk culture is born.

In most parts of China, flying kite is done in the spring and autumn because of wind and farming practice. During spring and autumn, wind speed is good for outdoor activities, while it is too hot in summer, with thunder and storms. Winter is cold when temperature is low and strong wind keeps changing directions. This leaves only spring and autumn good for kite flying. As an agricultural country, people farmed by seasons and recreation was only done when working is slack during the tenth and the fourth month of the next year by traditional Chinese calendar, during which time, apart from repairing farming tools, people make kites to fly.

在此时开始制作风筝。

至开春季节，天气变暖，东风渐急，农事当闲，草木未苏，气候、时间、场地都有利于风筝的放飞。特别是在北方的产麦区，由于此时麦子没有发棵，不怕踩，因而人们可以在广阔的麦田上奔跑着放风筝。

春天放风筝在中医学上也有据可循。中医认为冬天人们多待在室内，积攒了一冬的内热，而在春天外出放风筝，可以疏泄内热，舒展筋骨，增强体质。

After spring comes, when cold weather is over and wind from east comes at a moderate speed, when farming activities are not many and vegetations back to life, everything works for a favorable situation for kite flying. Even more so, before wheat sprouts, people in the north were not hesitant to step in fields. They could run at will in vast countryside. Also, there was a reason from traditional Chinese medicine to encourage kite flying in the spring.

After staying inside through winter, people had inner heat in their bodies and flying kite outdoor might help release it. This was good for health. In China's south, particularly in coastal areas, rainfall was much in the spring. So kite flying was often seen on the Chongyang

• 年画《放风筝》（清）
此年画描绘了一对母女放风筝的情景。女孩拿着缠绕风筝线的轴作奔跑状，母亲则双手托着一只鲜艳的金鱼风筝，以协助放飞。
Flying Kite, New Year Painting (Qing Dynasty)
Mother and daughter are seen flying a kite. The daughter is running with a roller in hand, while her mother helps the gold-fish kite with her hands.

● 春天放风筝图 (图片提供：微图)
Flying the Kite in Spring

而在中国南方的许多地区，尤其是沿海一带，因春季雨水多，放风筝则更多是选在秋高气爽的重阳节，并与登高、郊游等活动结合在一起。

风筝放飞时的仪式也是风筝民俗文化的组成部分，其随着各地区风俗民情的差别而各不相同。在一些地方，风筝放飞前需要举行隆重的祭祀仪式，要将风筝先在全村游行展示，后供奉于香案上，接受全村男子的叩拜，以祈祷风调雨顺、五谷丰收，最后风筝才可以被放

Festival, when people did outing or climbing a hill.

The ceremony for kite flying shows the custom of a place. In some places, people will show the kites around the village, worshipped on a table by all men before it was sent to the sky. This is to get a good harvest that year. In other places, people will write their names on a kite, and after it is in the sky cut the thread and let it go, supposedly to take away a bad luck. The ceremony held in Jiangsu and Zhejiang is more ceremonial. A couple of days in

● 风筝放飞仪式中数十人共同举着风筝（图片提供：FOTOE）
Tens of People Hold the Kite to Send It into Sky.

飞。也有些地方，人们会在风筝上写上自己的名字，待风筝放飞后，剪断引线，让风筝随风飘去，以达到消灾祛难的目的。在江浙一带，人们非常重视板鹞风筝的放飞，一般会提前准备数日，向风筝敬献祭品。放飞时则由数十个青年男子共同放飞，风筝一飞冲天，预示着一年的丰收。之后，男女老少会举行庆祝风筝成功放飞的酒宴，人们一面品尝菜肴，一面赏听板鹞从空中发出的乐声，场面热闹而欢快。

advance, a worshipping ceremony is held with sacrifices. On the day, dozens of young men work together sending the kite into the sky. This is an omen for a good harvest that year. Then, people will gather for a feast, while enjoying the sound from the whistles on the kite.

风筝分类
Category of Kites

　　风筝多种多样，人们主要以形态、大小、功能和结构四项标准来划分风筝的类别。

There are many varieties of kites, categorized by shape, size, function and structure.

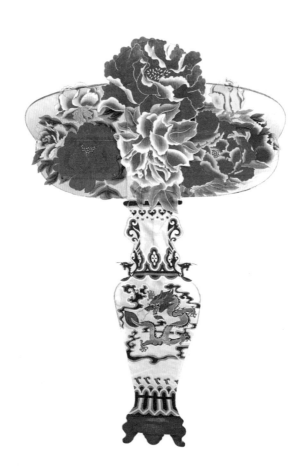

> 风筝的形态

　　风筝按形状可分为人物形风筝、动物形风筝、植物形风筝、物品类风筝、字形风筝，以及几何形状的风筝等。

　　人物形状的风筝多以神话人物为主要表现题材，包括美猴王孙悟空、仙女嫦娥、道教神话人物麻

> The Shape of Kites

Some kites are in the shape of human beings, animals, plants, and things used in life, Chinese characters and geometrical shapes.

　　Some kites have the characters from classical novels or tales like the Monkey King, fairy Chang'e, Magu of Taoism, immortals Zhong Kui and Liu Hai able

• 硬翅风筝《钟馗》 罗焕文制
钟馗是中国传统文化中的"赐福镇宅圣君"，被奉为吉神。此风筝上的钟馗相貌奇异，铁面虬鬓，身着绘有神兽麒麟的官袍，身后背着宝剑，作跳舞状。
Ghost Buster Zhong Kui, Hard-wing Kite, Made by Luo Huanwen

Zhong Kui is held in traditional culture as a god able to bring good luck. He has a very frightening looks, clad in an official robe with magic animal Qilin, carrying a sword on his back, often painted in a dancing position.

- 风筝《孙悟空》

  孙悟空是中国四大名著之一《西游记》中的角色，会七十二变、腾云驾雾。在此风筝的两翼和尾巴处均画有站在云彩上的孙悟空，形象地表现出孙悟空的特点。

  Monkey King **Kite**

  The Monkey King is a character from the classical novel *Journey to the West*. Monkey King has magic skills, able to fly and change forms. His image on the tips of kite wings and tail are so vivid like standing on a cloud.

姑、能驱鬼辟邪的神仙钟馗和财神刘海等。其形式有人物与文字组合而成，也有人物与动物结合在一起，如著名的山东潍坊风筝《仙鹤童子》表现的就是骑在仙鹤上的童子图案。

动物形状的风筝以动物为基础形态，放飞时运用放飞技巧使风筝模拟老鹰、沙燕、蝙蝠、金鱼、龙凤、蝴蝶等动物模样，具有很强的

to dispel bad lucks. The former is a ghost buster while the later, god of fortunes. Some human figures are painted together with written characters, while some, with animals. "Crane and Boy", famous pattern from Weifang of Shandong Province, is very popular.

Some kites are made into animal shapes like an eagle, swallow, bat, gold fish, dragon, phoenix or butterfly. They are very enjoyable to look at. Most of

观赏性。动物风筝大多寓意吉祥，如寓意"福"的蝙蝠风筝，寓意"禄"的鹿形风筝等。在中国传统文化中占有独特地位的龙、凤也是动物风筝的主要题材之一。而寓意爱情美好、家庭圆满的鸳鸯、双沙燕、双鱼等也是动物风筝的常见题材。

植物形状的风筝图案主要是花卉类，如素有"百花之王"美称的牡丹和有"四君子"之称的梅、

them possess an auspicious message like bat and deer. The dragon and phoenix are frequently found in a traditional pattern, while mandarin ducks, swallows or twin-fish are also frequent patterns, suggesting romantic love or a happy family life.

Most flower kites are made in the shape of peony, "king of the flowers", and plum, orchid, bamboo and chrysanthemum, "the four gentlemen", very beautiful to look at and containing much cultural message. These four stand

• 风筝《五龙》 哈亦琦制

龙不仅是中国的传统吉祥神兽，也是权利和皇家的象征，中国封建皇帝尊崇龙，自喻为龙的化身。此风筝上面共画有五条龙，在风筝的中间位置为红色的正龙，两翼及两尾上则为四条颜色不同的降龙。

Kite *Five Dragons*, Made by Ha Yiqi

Not only held as magic, the dragon was also a symbol of royal family. All the emperors in ancient Chinese history worshipped dragon, taking themselves as descendents of the dragon. This kite has five dragons on it, the red one at the center indicating the ruler, while the four around in different colors, its subordinates.

• 长尾平头风筝《鲇鱼》

此鲇鱼风筝为典型的长尾平头风筝，圆形的头采用硬面结构，以使其受强风而不变形，下部为软面的飘带式长尾，放飞时能随风产生摇头摆尾的美妙动态。

Catfish, Kite with Long Tail and Level Head

This hard-structured kite is designed to fly in a bigger wind. The long tail waves in the air like what fish does in water.

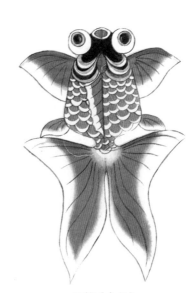

• 风筝《金鱼》
Gold Fish Kite

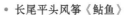

• 风筝《蝴蝶》
Butterfly Kite

中国龙形风筝的扎制

　　要制作一只龙形风筝，需要许多道工序。首先，龙头需由100多种不同的竹条捆扎而成，骨架外面还要按其形状糊上一块块绢料。龙嘴里的牙齿用泡沫塑料刻制而成，舌头用混凝纸浆做成。眉毛以及会转动的双眼栩栩如生，胡子则绘制成鲜艳的红色。其次，龙身的制造较为复杂，需将细竹条弯成圆形，并用线绑扎成多个圆箍连接起来，外面糊上施以彩画的绢绸，再捆上末端加有羽毛的竹条作为龙爪。最后，将组成龙身的圆盘分别固定在绳子上，并用钩子将龙身与龙头相接，龙形风筝便可放飞到空中了。

● 放飞在天空中的龙形风筝（图片提供：微图）
Dragon Kite in the Sky

Dragon Kite Making

It takes many steps to make a dragon kite. First, over a hundred bamboo slips are bound together before pasted with silk as a cover. The dragon teeth are made with foamed plastic, its tongue, hard paper pulp. It has moveable eyes and eyebrows. It has long and red whiskers. It is more difficult to make its body: very thin bamboo strips are bent into circles connected together, covered with color silk on top before receiving claws made with feathered bamboo strips. All the circles are fixed onto a rope, a hook connects the body and head before the dragon is ready to fly.

兰、竹、菊。风筝上的梅、兰、竹、菊纹饰不仅图案美观，而且寓意高洁的品质。它们的品质分别是梅傲、兰幽、竹坚、菊淡，共同特点为自强不息，清华其外，淡泊其中，不作媚世之态。正是由于这种高雅的品性和人们对于高尚境界的神往，梅、兰、竹、菊便成为中国人借物明志的象征，也是风筝上文人画中较为常见的题材。蔬菜类的白菜、胡萝卜等造型也较为常见，这种风筝既与人们的日常生活密切相关，又是人们借助谐音祈求吉祥的体现，如白菜风筝的"菜"与"财"谐音，寓意富贵常在。

物品类的风筝以日常生活器物为造型来源，如钟形风筝、扇形风

for a proud, loft and detached personality refusing to yield to worldliness. This characteristic is admired in traditional culture. And because plum, orchid, bamboo and chrysanthemum are associated with these characteristic they are favored patterns for kites, often done by a scholar painter. Chinese cabbage and carrots are also favored subject because they are homophones of good luck and fortune in Chinese language, also because they are closely related to daily life.

Kites may also be made like a clock, fan, lantern used inside a royal palace or a vase. The kites in the shape of a clock have highly symmetrical parts decorated with impressive lines, looking stately and solemn. Kites made like a lantern used inside a palace often have a 3-D

• 植物风筝《吉祥花篮》

此风筝整体呈花篮的形状，花篮上方为八朵五颜六色的牡丹花，下方是红色的长穗，装饰效果明显。

Flower Basket, Plant Kite

This kite is made like a flower basket holding colorful peony. The lower part has highly decorative long laces in red.

• 植物风筝《富贵牡丹》

此风筝的形制为装在花瓶中的牡丹花，寓意富贵的牡丹和花瓶上象征权力、地位的龙形图案共同组成了一幅富贵牡丹图。另外，在花瓶的底部还设计了一个支撑花瓶的凳子，使风筝的形象更加逼真。

Noble Peony, Plant Kite

This kite is made like peony inside a vase. Together with the dragon, symbol of power, it is a nice patter for fortune and good luck. At the bottom of the vase is a stool, which makes the whole pattern vivid.

筝、宫灯风筝和花篮风筝等。其中，钟形风筝多采用对称的外形，装饰以华丽的龙纹，具有很强的庄重感。宫灯风筝采用立体结构扎制，放飞到空中，能够呈现出摇曳的姿态，如风中的明灯一般。

字形风筝是风筝制作与中国汉字相结合的创新型风筝，既有文字与实物的组合，又有单独的文字造型，并多以"寿"、"喜"等吉祥文字为主。寿字形风筝是以"寿"字和寿星、仙女等神话人物相结合而构成的形神兼备的作品。喜字形风筝分为"喜"字和"双喜"字两种。

structure, able to dance in air or to light in dark sky.

Fans made in the shape of a written character are a fairly new type. They may have just a character, or a character and something else. Frequently used characters are "longevity", "happiness". The kites with "longevity" may have the image of longevity god and fairies. The kites with "happiness" may have one character, or two characters, "double happiness". "Double happiness" in red

• **扇形风筝**

中国具有深厚的扇文化底蕴，历来有"制扇王国"的美誉。此扇形风筝采用中国传统的折扇形式，扇面上画着由花朵、枝叶组成的折枝花卉。

Kite in the Shape of Fan

Fan making has a long history in China, which is called "kingdom of fan making" in the world. This kite is like a foldable fan, with flowers and leaves painted on its face.

红色双喜字是中国传统剪纸的常见造型，是婚礼中不可缺少的装饰元素。双喜字以文字"喜"为造型基础，装饰以梅、兰、竹、菊等纹样，既喜庆，又含有丰富的寓意。

often appears on a wedding, a much favored pattern for paper cutting. Kites with this pattern may also have plum, orchid, bamboo or chrysanthemum to go with, very festival and meaningful.

• **"双喜"字风筝**
在此双喜字形状的风筝上面有牡丹花、菊花和喇叭花等花卉图案。
Kite with "Double Happiness"
Peony, chrysanthemum and flowers of other kind appear on this kite characteristic with "double happiness".

风筝与婚姻礼俗

中国古代的婚娶礼俗中包含着求子祈嗣的寓意，多子多福的婚俗观念始终贯穿在婚娶的过程中。如人们在为新娘缝制被褥时，一般会缝上枣子、花生、桂圆、栗子等图案，象征早生贵子。这种祈求儿女满堂的婚姻礼俗反映到风筝中就是麒麟送子、仙鹤送子、榴开百子等风筝的出现。风筝是表现婚姻礼俗的极好载体，关于贺喜方面的风筝有数十种。天仙配风筝、牛郎织女风筝、梁祝风筝、鸳鸯风筝、比翼鸟风筝、龙凤呈祥风筝等，都是用来表达对新郎、新娘的美好祝愿的。此类风筝不但用于放飞，而且做工精致，可作为贺礼赠送给新婚夫妇。

Kites and Wedding Customs

Traditional weddings in ancient China were very emphatic on the prospect of getting more sons, a very important wish seen in all the steps. When beddings were made for the newlyweds, images of date, peanut, longan and chestnut was embroidered on the cover. They were symbol of getting sons as early as possible. Images associated with this idea were "Qilin delivering baby", "crane delivering a boy infant" and "pomegranate seeds". Kites made a nice vehicle for this belief. Popular varieties were dozens, "Niulang and Zhinv", "Liang Shanbo and Zhu Yingtai", "mandarin ducks", "male and female birds flying together", so on and so forth. These elaborately made kites carried the best wishes for the newlyweds. They could fly, also made a nice present on a wedding.

• 软翅风筝《瓜瓞绵绵》 费保龄制
此风筝将蝴蝶、瓜、藤蔓、葫芦、蝙蝠组合在一起，寓意子孙众多、繁荣昌盛。

Continuous Small Melons, Soft-wing Kite, Made by Fei Baoling

This kite has a combination of butterfly, melon, vine, gourd and bat, all symbolizing prosperous descendents.

几何形状的风筝包括多边形、八卦形风筝等。多边形风筝有三边、四边、五边、六边等形状，这种风筝外形简单，容易制成，是一种常见的风筝。八卦风筝为多种图案组合而成的几何形风筝，以道教八卦为造型基础，装饰有道教人物图案，形态富于变化。

Kites in geometrical shapes also have different types. Some have three, four, five, even six sides. Kites of this type are easy to make, very popular in society. The Eight-diagram kites may contain five different images from Taoism. Taoist figures make this type of kites lively and full of change.

● 三角形风筝（图片提供：全景正片）
Triangular Kite

> 风筝的大小

　　风筝按大小可分为巨型风筝、大型风筝、中型风筝、小型风筝和微型风筝。巨型风筝是指面积在10平方米以上，或者串式风筝100节以上的一切形体巨大的风筝，如中国南通的大板鹞、潍坊的龙头蜈蚣风筝等。大型风筝指面积在2平方米以上，或串式风筝50节以上的形体较大的风筝。中型风筝的面积在1平方米左右。小型风筝的面积为0.3—0.6平方米，这种风筝便于携带，也容易制作，很多娱乐风筝都是这种尺寸的。微型风筝是最小的风筝，面积在0.01平方米以下，因其形体很小，大多作为观赏风筝，但依然可以放飞，较为典型的微型风筝是微型沙燕风筝。

> The Size of Kites

By size, kites can be categorized into giant, large, medium, small and mini. "Giant" refers to the size over 10 square meters large, or having a string with over a hundred portions. Both Nantong and Weifang have giant bird kite or dragon-head centipede. Large kites are over 2 square meters in size or having portions over fifty. The medium size refers to about one square meter large and small size, only something between 0.3-0.6 square meters large. Most kites for entertainment fall in this category because it is easy to make and to carry along. Mini kites mean the kites smaller than 0.01 square meters. Because of their small size, most of them are for decoration. Small as it is, this category can fly too. The typical of this type is the swallow kite.

• 巨型风筝《龙头蜈蚣》 中国美术馆藏

龙头蜈蚣风筝以竹骨架扎制成龙头，身子以圆形为节点，两边装置竹条，并饰有羽毛，以模仿蜈蚣的百足之态。身体部分可长可短，长的可达百余节。

Giant Kite, *Centipede with Dragon's Head*, in the Collection of the National Art Museum of China

Centipede kites have dragon's head made with bamboo skin slips. Their body has slips bent into circles with other bamboo slips on each side, and decorated with feathers standing for the feet of a centipede. The length of the body may vary, some having a hundred sections.

- 微型风筝《蝴蝶》

  微型风筝以观赏为主，也可放飞，多采用薄棉纸制作而成，并用水彩色描绘成蝴蝶、沙燕等图案。

  Butterfly, Mini Kite

  Most mini kites are made with thin tissue paper and painted like a butterfly or swallow. Apart from being decorative, they can also fly.

- 中型风筝《肥燕》

  Fat Swallow, Medium-size Kite

> 风筝的功能

风筝按功能主要分为娱乐风筝、观赏风筝、特技风筝和实用风筝等。

娱乐风筝作为一种玩具，一般来说没有很高的艺术价值和特殊性能，但是制作简单、成本低廉、容易放飞和便于普及，是数量最多、流传最广的风筝品种。

观赏风筝的艺术价值较高，造型、图案、色彩和用材都十分考究。这类风筝来源于过去的宫廷风筝，造型优美，制作精巧，并在风筝的图案中融入诗、书、年画等多种艺术。观赏风筝集娱乐和观赏为一体，不仅可以放飞，而且可以作为工艺品来欣赏，即使挂在墙壁和橱窗上面，也是美观的装饰品。

> The Function of Kites

By their functions, kites can be categorized into "entertaining type", "decorative type", "special-effect type" and "practical-use type".

As a toy, the kite for entertainment, in most cases, doesn't have much artistic value or possibility for a special use. But they are simple to make, very inexpensive, easy to fly and to popularize. Most of the kites fall in this category.

Kites for decoration are beautifully painted and made with fine materials. This type of kites came from those inside royal palace in history. They are elaborately made, and often having a poem, a painting, or a piece of calligraphic work on their body. Apart from flying, this type is often beautiful handicraft works found on walls or windows as nice decoration.

- 娱乐风筝《娃娃》

此娱乐风筝的形状为一个女娃的头像，其图案简单，人物的眉毛、眼睛、鼻了等的刻画均较为粗略，在眉心和头上绑有三根风筝线，易于放飞。

Baby, Kite for Entertainment

This kite is a baby girl's head, with briefly painted eyebrows, eyes and nose. It has three threads from its eyebrows and head, easy to fly.

- 观赏风筝《舞剑美人》

此风筝的图案为正在舞剑的美人，美人上身穿桃红色敞口短衣，下穿白色长裙，左手持剑，右手举起，作挥舞状，身姿轻盈如燕，似点剑而起。风筝图案绘制精美，人物惟妙惟肖，是观赏类风筝中的佳作。

Sword Dancing Beauty, Decorative Kite

The beauty in a red blouse over white dress has a sword in her left hand, lifting her right hand in a very graceful dancing position. This beautiful image makes this kite highly enjoyable to view.

年画对风筝的影响

　　年画等民间艺术对风筝的影响是显而易见的，很多年画在社会上流行多年，深受人们的喜爱，因而年画的内容甚至是名字都被移植到风筝上面。如《吉庆有余》风筝、《新春牛图》风筝等，从图案内容到名字都与年画的相同。而且，风筝的绘制大多与年画的绘画风格结合起来，如潍坊杨家埠风筝实际上是杨家埠木版年画与风筝扎制艺术的结合体，人们将印制好的木版年画剪贴在扎好的风筝骨架上，便可得到一件完整美观的风筝。

Influence on Kites from New Year Painting

The influence from New Year painting is very obvious on kites, particularly from paintings popular for many years. Apart from similar images, some kites simply take the titles from these paintings, examples being *Happiness and Festivity*, *Ox Plowing in Spring*. Paintings on kites are almost the same with those of the New Year paintings. The kites from Yangjiabu, Weifang, are a fine example for the combination of the two. People there simply paste a finished painting on the skeleton of a kite and it is done.

● **蘑菇伞风筝《八仙》**

八仙指中国神话传说中的汉钟离、张果老、韩湘子、铁拐李、吕洞宾、曹国舅、蓝采和、何仙姑八位神仙。他们各有一件法宝，神通广大，能为百姓除疾苦，因此深受人们的喜爱，是年画和风筝中的常见题材。

Eight Immortals, Mushroom-umbrella Kite

The eight immortals are popular figures in Chinese mythology. They are Zhang Guolao, Han Xiangzi, Iron Crutch Li, Lv Dongbin, Cao Guojiu, Lan Caihe and He Xiangu. Each has a magic weapon, with which they help poor people in need. People love their stories, so they are often seen in New Year Paintings and kites.

特技风筝主要注重风筝的特技性能，在制作技术和放飞技巧上都需要特别设计，使其可以在空中旋转翻飞、变色、放烟火、撒彩纸、发光等。中国自宋代就有斗风筝的习俗，这类风筝在制作上用双线或多线代替普通风筝中的单线；风筝放飞时两手操控风筝线，来改变风筝的飞行方向，以使风筝前进、倒退、旋转、翻滚和多向飞行。有的风筝可以随意停止或是前进，还能够配合音乐进行表演。还有一类风筝可以进行一些情景表演，如传统的《来回送饭》风筝可以在风筝放飞稳定时将彩带等装饰送至风筝高处，而外形为飞机形状的新型飞机风筝能做出射击、放降落伞等特技表演。另外，人们也利用新材料制

Special effect kites are specially designed and made for a functioning purpose. They are able to turn, whirl, spit fire or smoke, spread color paper, and even give off light in the air. Kites fight, a game starting from the Song Dynasty, uses special effect kites with two or even more threads to control. The person who flies it uses both hands to operate. By the threads, he can make the kite in the air move forward and back, stop, turn, roll, and fly in different directions. Some kites can move to music. Still some can perform a story in the air, like "the kite coming and going to deliver food" is able to bring color ribbons well up into sky. New performance kites in the shape of an airplane can shoot and release parachutes. New materials are used to give different light. This kind is lighter and brighter in

● **特技风筝《来回送饭》**

"来回送饭"风筝又称为"风筝碰"，上面安装有附加装置，可以在风筝放飞时将彩纸、灯笼等装饰物放在小盒子内沿着风筝线送到空中，小盒子在碰到风筝后可撒下彩带等，如同仙女散花一般，场面十分壮观。

Special Effect Kite, *Coming and Going to Deliver Food*

Kites of this type, called *feng zheng pen*, have special installations. They carry color paper and lanterns in small boxes. Up into sky, when the boxes bump into the kite, color paper clips and ribbons come out, like a fairy maiden spreading flowers.

● **特技风筝**（图片提供：微图）
Special Effect Kite

作出可发出不同光芒的风筝，颜色多样而且载重轻，夜晚时长长的彩带在空中随风而动，美不胜收。

实用风筝能够完成一定的工作任务，可以进行空中摄影、通讯、宣传、救生、科研、气象勘测，或者用来充当无线电天线牵引车船等。风筝不仅在中国具有实用功能，世界上的许多国家也都利用风筝来完成特定的工作。如在第二次世界大战中，英国曾利用风筝监视德国潜艇，还曾把风筝作为防空装置配置在驱逐舰上。

color, very beautiful in an evening sky with long ribbons drifting behind.

Kites for practical use may undertake a special mission like air photography, communication, broadcasting a message, salvation, sci-tech research, weather investigation, or serve as antenna for vehicles and boats. Not only in China, have some other countries used kites for these purposes. During World War Two, Britain used kites to keep watch on German submarines. They even had some on their destroyers as an anti-aircraft device.

> 风筝的结构

　　风筝一般是以竹料为骨架，根据风筝扎制过程中竹骨架扎制的不同结构，可把风筝分为软翅类、硬翅类、拍子、串式、伞翼、立体等类别。

　　软翅风筝指风筝翅膀的上方为竹条、下方是软边的风筝。其主体

> The Structure of Kites

Most kites are made with bamboo for structures. These kites are in different types, those with soft wings, hard wings, flat, stringed, like an umbrella or in three dimensions.

　　The kites with soft wings often have bamboo slips on top and soft materials below. Their main structure is often

● 软翅风筝《鹰》
Eagle, Soft-wing Kite

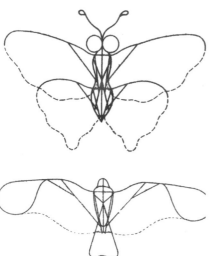

- 软翅风筝结构图
  The Structure of Soft-wing Kite

- 软翅风筝《蜻蜓》
  软翅风筝的翅膀下方没有竹条固定，所以放飞时翅膀随风而动，十分轻灵飘逸。
  Dragonfly, Soft-wing Kite
  Their wings have no bamboo slips, so they are light in air and can move wings in wind.

- 软翅风筝《蝴蝶》
  Butterfly, Soft-wing Kite

骨架做成浮雕式，骨架为单层的、双层的或多层的，裱糊材质为绢或现代新型纤维，并采用写实的手法描绘图案。这类风筝起飞比较容易，是民间常见的风筝，适合扎制老鹰、金鱼、蝴蝶、蜻蜓等飞禽、昆虫类型的风筝，形象逼真。如飞鸟风筝放飞时模拟飞鸟飞行盘旋的姿态，软翅随风扇动，神态生动；金鱼风筝放飞时胸鳍、尾鳍飘动，如在水中漫游。

硬翅风筝的翅膀上下均有竹条，翅膀由竖长方形固定，两翅

carved, some having one layer, others having two or even more. The soft materials used are often silk or new-type fiber, with painted images in realistic style. These kites are popular and easy to fly. Most often seen are dragonflies, goldfish, butterflies, eagles and insects painted truthfully. Bird kites can twirl in the air and their soft wings can flap. Goldfish kites have movable pectoral and tail fins, just like what fish do in water.

Hard-wing kites have a bamboo slip structure in rectangular shape on wings, higher on edge and lower at the center. Their tips are made like a triangle

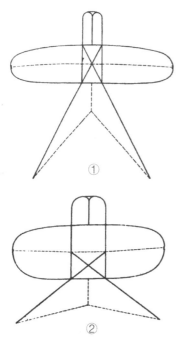

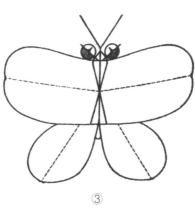

• 硬翅风筝结构图
The Structure of Hard-wing Kite

- 硬翅风筝《秦琼》 赵铁民制

  秦琼是唐代名将，为人豪爽耿直，因其正气威武，被人们奉为门神，用来镇宅辟邪。此风筝上的秦琼头戴宝盔，身穿官服，手拿长枪，形象生动传神。风筝骨架采用米字形的硬翅风筝结构，边缘上有竹条支撑。

  Warrior Qin Qiong, Hard-wing Kite, Made by Zhao Tiemin

  Qin Qiong, a warrior during the Tang Dynasty, was a righteous man who valued brotherhood more than anything else. Because of him, people said, evil spirits stayed away so he was taken as a door god to keep a house safe. On this kite, he wears a helmet and an official robe, holding a spear in hand, very life-like. The kite structure has hard wings made in double crosses with bamboo slips to support edges.

- 硬翅风筝
  Hard-wing Kite

边缘高，中间略凹，端部后倾，使风从两翅的端部溢出，形成三角兜风。其基本骨架有沙燕、米字形、多层硬翅三种。沙燕是北京传统风筝骨架形态，分为瘦沙燕和肥沙燕两种。米字形骨架适用于多种题材的风筝，像人物、飞鸟、兽类、昆虫类风筝都可以使用这种结构扎制。多层硬翅形骨架由多层硬翅构成，青蛙、蝴蝶、字形、塔形、器物形风筝多采用这种骨架结构。

拍子风筝即人们所说的平面形风筝，包括硬拍子风筝和软拍子风筝。硬拍子风筝的中间和四周为竹

to catch wind force. Kites of this type have three basic forms: the swallow, double crisscross and multiple layers. The swallow type is typical in Beijing, but still, they fall into two kinds, skinny and fat. The double cross type is good for images of man, birds, animals and insects, while the multiple layer type has harder wings, good for the images of frogs, butterflies, Chinese written characters, pagodas and other things.

Flat kites also fall into two types, the soft and hard. The hard ones have bamboo slips in the middle and edges, no thread on the back of the bent body. Its structure is in two types, flat and semi-

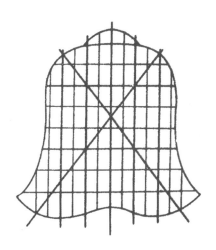

• 硬拍子风筝的结构图
The Structure of Hard-wing Flat Kite

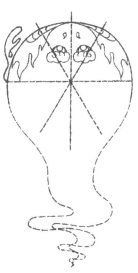

• 软拍子风筝的结构图
The Structure of Soft-wing Flat Kite

* 拍子风筝《海屋添筹》 周树堂制

海屋添筹指的是神话传说中居于海岛之上的神仙不计时间，每当看到人间的沧海变成桑田时便把一根筹置于房中，因一筹代表千岁而寓意长寿。此风筝的主体为上下两层的海屋，海屋位于海水之上，四面围绕着象征长寿的仙鹤。风筝骨架为平面形的拍子风筝结构，中间受风，两边泄风。

The Immortal Who Keeps Track of Time with Sticks, Flat Kite, Made by Zhou Shutang

The Immortal Who Keeps Track of Time with Sticks is a folk story. It tells an immortal, after seeing the huge change that happens in human world, keeps track of it with a stick erected in his dwelling place. One stick stands for a thousand years that have passed. This kite has a two-story house on water, with cranes around to stand for longevity. Its structure is flat to receive wind in the middle and release air on sides.

条，背后不用线，而将整个风筝面拉成弓形，骨架分平面和半立体两种。这类风筝扎制容易，平衡性好，易于放飞。尾部系长绳或串穗的风筝都属此类，包括龙凤瓶风筝、葫芦风筝等。软拍子风筝同硬拍子风筝一样，中间和四周有竹条，但背后需用线将整个风筝面拉紧成弓形。其适用于多种题材，如八卦风筝、鱼虫、器物风筝等。

串式风筝是把几个或是多至几百个风筝用一根或多根线连接在一

three-dimensional. This type of kites is easy to make and fly and balances well in the air. All kites with a thread or laces on their tails, including "dragon and phoenix" and "gourd". The soft, like the hard ones, also has bamboo slips in the middle and edges threads on the back bend it into the right shape. This kind of kites are good for multiple themes like "the eight diagrams", "fish and insects" and things used in daily life.

String kites may have several or several hundred individual kites strung together by a thread, very powerful and

起的风筝。这类风筝气势宏大，具有生动活泼的艺术表现力，包括多个风筝连成一串的软翅节风筝，如串雁；以及多个不同风筝拼接成一个风筝形象，如潍坊的蜈蚣风筝。

伞翼风筝以三角形骨架为支撑，或是无骨架而拉成弧形的各种形体的软风筝，也指将以上两种结构组合而成的风筝。其优点是制

spectacular to see in air. They may be made like a string of swallows or wild geese. In Weifang, people make this kite by combining different types, like they do for a centipede one.

Parasol-wing kites may have structures in triangular form, or without a skeleton but stretched into arcs to form soft wings. This type also includes two different structures. They are easy

- 串式风筝《京剧脸谱》（图片提供：微图）
  京剧脸谱是具有中国特色的一种特殊的化妆方法，由于每个历史人物或某一种类型的人物都有一种大概的谱式，所以称为"脸谱"。此风筝由数十个绘有京剧脸谱的风筝用线连接而成，放飞时的场面逼真生动。

Peking Opera String Kite

Peking Opera masks are unique, each standing for a type of characters and this has been stereotyped. This kite has tens of masks, strung together by a thread. In the air, they look quite impressive.

- 伞翼风筝《孔雀开屏》

伞翼风筝多利用现代纤维材料制作而成，形态多样，色彩艳丽，体积大。此风筝形象地将孔雀开屏时五彩缤纷、色泽艳丽的尾屏展现出来。

Peacock Shows Its Tail, Parasol-wing Kite

Most kites of this type are made with modern fiber materials, which give possibilities for more appearances, colors and sizes. This one shows a peacock spreading its colorful tail.

作简单，易于表现人物、动物、植物、几何形体等各种题材，且起飞性能好。

立体风筝指非平面风筝，一般采用折叠结构的骨架，可单只放飞或成双放飞。中国传统的桶形风筝即是立体风筝，由一个或多个圆

to make, very good for the images of a human, animal, plants or geometric shapes. They are easy to take off.

Three-dimensional kites are not flat, but have foldable structures, able to fly individually or in pair. Traditional kites of this type are like a barrel, or more barrels strung together. Examples are

● 立体风筝《逗鸟人》
此风筝的形象为一个中年男子一担挑两只圆筒状的鸟笼，鸟笼内隐约可见翠鸟的影子，立体造型使风筝的形象更为直观。
Man Teasing Bird, a 3-D Kite

This kite has a man carrying two barrels by a shoulder pole. Inside the barrels are kingfisher birds faintly visible. Three dimensions make this kite more vivid and life-like.

● 立体风筝《老鼠娶亲》 杨红卫制
此风筝取材于民间的"老鼠娶亲"故事。风筝将老鼠的形态拟人化，采用立体的方式展现了四只老鼠抬着喜轿的场景，老鼠神情庄重，别有意味。
Mouse' Wedding, 3-D Kite, Made by Yang Hongwei
This image comes from a legend. The four mice are personified for a 3-D effect. They look solemn, a very amusing picture.

桶组成，如宫灯、花瓶、酒瓶等风筝。山东潍坊曾放飞过"鲤鱼跳龙门"的巨型立体风筝，创造了当时最长和最大风筝的吉尼斯世界纪录。

palace lanterns, flower vases and wine bottles. A huge kite of this type, "carp fish leaping over *Longmen* (dragon gate)" made in Weifang, Shandong Province, was taken into the Guinness record as the longest and the biggest of the time in the world.

风筝工艺
Making Techniques

　　风筝的制作工序多达十几道，包括设计、选材、整形、绑扎、裁剪、绘画、装配、拴脚线、试飞、调整等。经过长期的反复制作与总结，中国民间手工艺人将此概括为"扎、糊、绘、放"四艺。

It takes over ten steps to make a kite, including designing, material selecting, shaping, binding, tailoring, painting, assembling, threading, test flying and adjusting. Over the past hundreds of years, Chinese kite makers have summarized the steps into four kinds of techniques, respectively called structuring, Mounting, painting and flying.

> 风筝的扎制

制作风筝首先要考虑的是风筝骨架的扎制，一般要经过选、劈、削、弯、接五道工序。

选：中国传统风筝骨架扎制的选材多以竹子为主材，以苇子、高粱秆做辅料。扎制风筝时经常使用的竹子有毛竹、桂竹、水竹、慈竹等。毛竹材质坚韧，分布地区范围广，是制作各类风筝的良好材料。桂竹材质坚硬，柔韧性好，多用于制作风筝主骨。水竹竿直，质地坚密，韧性好，是制作大小风筝细部骨架的好材料。慈竹质地柔软，材质轻，适合制作中型风筝的直杆。

劈：由于竹的纹理平直，因此可用劈的方法沿竹的自然纹理将其撕开。劈竹前要对圆竹进行加工，去掉竹根和竹梢，截成1—1.5米长的

> Structuring

Structuring refers to the shaping of its structure, done by five steps, material selection, chopping, cutting, bending and connecting.

Material selection: Most of the materials are bamboo slips and reed or sorghum stalks as supplements. The often used four varieties are moso bamboo, fish scale bamboo, phyllostachys heteroclada, sinocalamus affinis. They are easy to find and they make good materials for kite making. Moso bamboo is strong and plastic, found in most parts of the country and often used for kite making. Fish scale bamboo is both tough and soft, ideal for making the structure. Phyllostachys heteroclada is straight, dense in quality and supple, very good for the rest parts of the kite. Sinocalamus affinis is light and strong, good for the axle of the structure for a medium-sized kite.

• 风筝制作材料中的水竹

作为扎制风筝骨架的主要材料，水竹要选择经过自然干燥的成年竹竿的中部。

Phyllostachys heteroclada for Kite Making

The central part of this bamboo variety, after growing up, is used after air dried for the kite structure.

• 劈竹

劈竹时可以把竹子的内竹节削去，但外竹节不能去除，以免造成竹子的断裂。

Bamboo Chopping

It means to remove the inside joints. The outside joints should be kept to keep the bamboo strong.

圆竹段，再把竹段劈成八块宽度大约相同的竹板待用。

削：用刀刃加工劈好的竹条，使之成为适合制作风筝各部件的材料。需要用削刮手法制作不同厚度、宽度和斜度的竹条。

弯：利用蜡烛或酒精灯熏烤加热的方法，使竹子变软，以达到弯曲所需的角度，并将弯曲后的竹子

Chopping: Because of bamboo's vertical veins, shopping easily gets slips. But before chopping, bamboo must be processed by removing roots and leaves, cut into sections between 1 to 1.5 meters long. Each section is then cut into eight boards of the same width.

Cutting: Cut the boards into slips of desired length, width and thickness for different parts of a kite. Different hand

浸入冷水中使之定型。弯是风筝定型的重要一步，加热的温度、时间和手劲大小要相配适中。

连接：把定型后的各部组件连接成一个整体，连接方式有固定和拆装两种。固定方式就是用条状的线、麻皮、纸和纺织品，通过垂直、倾斜和平行三种连接方式固定各部骨架。垂直连接有交叉接、卡接和搭接三种。交叉接方法简单，一般用"十"字绑扎法，但连接成的骨架不平，而且强度不大。卡接

• 劈好的竹条
Finished Bamboo Slips

moves give different thickness, width and inclination.

Bending: Heat bamboo slips until it is supple enough before bending them into required shape and left in cold water for finalization. Bending is crucial, for the heating temperature, timing and force applied make difference between success and failure.

Connecting: Assemble all the parts in ideal shape by either fixation or assembling. Fixation means to fix permanently each part with threads, hemp, paper or fabric in vertical, slanting or level way. Vertical connection may have different ways to do it, the most popular is binding into a cross but this way is not level enough and less strong. Another way is to cut a slip on end for fixation onto another. This way gives a fairly level surface. Still another way is to bend a slip 90 degrees to connect another one. This way gives a pleasant look but the length of the cut must be 6 times as much as the thickness of the slip before strength is guaranteed. Strong as it is, the two slips are not on the same level.

Structuring may be also assembled. This way is dismountable by using joints called *kouxie, huotou and chajie*. *Kouxie* was invented by Wei Yuantai in

要将一根竹条劈开，卡在另一根竹条上，骨架比交叉接平整。搭接时要有一根竹条弯曲90度，从而使连接成的骨架具有较大强度。倾斜连接与垂直连接相似，只是角度不同。平行连接分为斜口接和搭口接。斜口接是将两根相接竹条互切斜口，对在一起，再绑扎，这样既平行又美观，但斜口的长度要在竹条厚度的六倍以上，才能保证骨架具有足够的强度。搭口接方法较为简单，但连接的两根竹条不在同一平面上。

拆装方式是手工艺人创造的灵活的扎制方式，包括扣楔、活头、插接等。扣楔由天津风筝名家魏元泰创造，是在纵向骨架上打孔，而横向骨架穿孔连接的方法，适合制作一些用于特技表演的风筝。活头用于风筝的折叠拆装，其构造是在两条搭接的竹条中间以一横轴相连，竹条两端各有一金属套环。套环松开，竹条可折；套环收紧，则两根竹条便像一根张开的竹条一样。插接方法专门用于可拆装的小部件，使用套管进行连接。

- 削竹

削竹的方法一般为"抽削"，即操作者左手拿竹板，右手刃向持刀，使刀刃成一定角度压在竹肉上来回刮削，即可将竹条削薄。

Bamboo Cutting

Holding a bamboo board in one's left hand and a blade in the right hand breadthways, the cutter scrapes the board by a fixed angle repeatedly until it becomes slips of ideal thickness.

Tianjin. It works like this: drilling holes on the skeleton first for the connection of a horizontal part. This way is good for making kites for performance. *Huotou* is for mounting and dismounting, using a vertical axle to connect two slips. On each end of a bamboo slip is a metal ring. When the ring is opened, the slip can be taken out. When fastened, the connected two slips become one. This method is good for dismounting small parts connected by tubes.

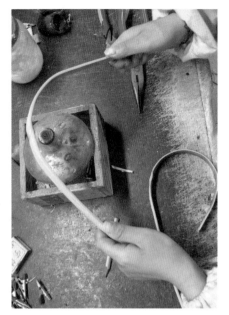

- 弯竹

  熏烤竹条时，竹条不能近距离接触火源，否则会将竹条烧焦。

  Bamboo Bending

  Bamboo slips should keep away from the source of heat when being bent, or they may get burnt.

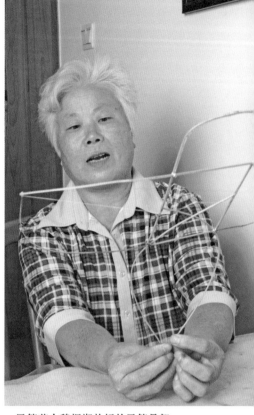

- 风筝艺人魏振湘扎好的风筝骨架

  魏振湘是著名的民间风筝艺人，曾获"伯乐杯"风筝比赛一等奖。

  Finished Structure, Made by Wei Zhenxiang

  Wei Zhenxiang is the famous folk kite artist, who once won the first prize of *Bole Cup* kite competition.

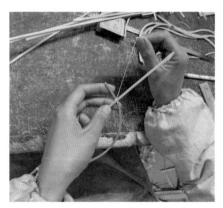

- 绑扎竹条

  Binding Bamboo Slips

风筝的制作工具

　　用于制作风筝的工具都比较普通、简易，大都是民间艺人根据自己的使用习惯自行制作，以方便好用为宜。基本上包括以下工具：

　　小刀和剪刀：用来削制竹材和裁剪纸张。

　　劈竹刀：用于将竹子劈开，除传统的厚背劈竹刀外，还可自制劈刀。找一段长约200毫米、宽50—60毫米、厚5毫米以上的钢板，且在其一端有一个直径约15毫米的孔，将此端钢板磨成一个斜角以形成刃口，再将钢棍插入孔洞，劈刀就做好了。它可以轻易劈开任何直径小于160毫米的大竹。

　　酒精灯：用于弯曲竹料。弯竹时若需要使酒精灯的灯焰平稳和适当提高温度，可加金属网罩。为避免烧焦，竹条还需在热源上来回移动。

　　钢丝钳：用来夹断铁丝，以将需要连接在一起的竹条绑扎起来。

　　胶水：以乳胶为佳。胶的浓度要根据所糊材料而定，材料薄则不要用强度大的胶水，要用稀一点的胶水，反之，则要求胶合强度大和浓度高的乳胶。一些骨架的角落里还不能积留很多胶水，以避免风筝表面不平整。

● 风筝的制作工具
Tools for Kite Making

Tools for Kite Making

Tools for kite making are simple, and often self-made by craftsmen for convenience, most often including the followings:

Small knife and a pair of scissors for scraping slips and cut paper.

Chopper: As its name suggests, it chops open bamboo. Apart from thick ones, craftsmen may make one for a special need with steel 200 mm long, between 50 and 60 mm wide and 5 mm thick. A hole is drilled at one end before grinding this end into an edge. The hole is to receive an iron bar. This chopper easily cuts open a bamboo 160 mm in diameter.

Alcohol lamp: This lamp heats bamboo slips for bending. Some lamps have a mesh screen of metal for a stable flame and regular heat. The slips keep moving while being heated. This is to avoid getting burnt.

Wire cutter: Cutting an iron wire for binding purpose.

Glue: Latex is the best. Concentration depends on the materials to be used for. If a material is thin, the glue should be thin; if the material is thick the glue, thicker. No glue should be left in corners in the structure because it affects smoothness of the surface.

• 风筝的制作工具
Tools for Kite Making

081
风筝工艺
Making Techniques

> 风筝的糊制

风筝的糊制是把彩绘的纸或绢糊在扎好的骨架上面，中国南方的风筝艺人称做"蒙面"，北方的称做"裱糊"，其包括选、裁、糊、边、校五道工序。

选：为不同规格和形状的风筝挑选合适的材料。一般情况下，糊风筝的材料应富有弹性和韧性，常

> Mounting

Mounting refers to paste painted paper or silk onto the structure. Craftsmen in the south call it "masking" while those in the north, "pasting". It involves five steps: material selection, cutting, pasting, edging and adjustment.

Material selection: Select right materials for the kite to be made. Usually, the material should be elastic

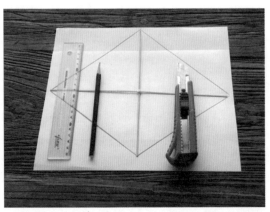

● **依风筝骨架画出纸型**

裁剪蒙面材料时，只要将其按照风筝图纸描绘出来即可。但对于复杂的风筝骨架，需要用另外一张纸放在骨架的对应部位，沿边缘剪下后制成纸样，再依照纸样绘在蒙面材料上。

The Paper Cut by Structure Design

Tailing the mounting material is done by a design. Due to the complicity of a structure, another piece of paper is placed on top of the corresponding part on the structure and is cut by following the shape. This copy is for surface painting.

● **将蒙面材料糊在风筝骨架上**

糊蒙面材料前，可用毛笔沾上胶水均匀地涂在风筝骨架上，以避免在骨架上积留过多的胶水，从而保持蒙面材料在晾干后的平整性。

Mounting Material Is Being Pasted onto the Structure

Before this, a writing brush is used to brush glue onto the structure. This delicate process is to avoid excessive glue left and to keep the shape neat.

用的有绢和纸。绢具有细密质轻、强度大、着色好的特点，是传统风筝蒙面的上好材料，但绢价格较高，很少用于娱乐风筝的制作。自纸张出现后，纸便直接取代绢而成为风筝蒙面的主要材料。纸张的选择与风筝的大小和裱糊部位有关。小型风筝使用轻薄的纸张，大型风筝需要多层纸张裱糊在一起，也有将绢裱在纸上，形成一种兼具两者

and tough, and paper and silk meet the need. Silk is light, dense, strong and easy to pick up colors, because of this, silk is nice material for traditional kites. But silk is expensive, seldom used for kites of entertainment before paper came into being. After replacing silk, paper quickly became the most popular material. The size of paper used is related to the parts and the size of a kite. Smaller kites use thinner and lighter paper, while big kites

特色的新型复合材料。近代科技的
发展促进了新材料的使用，出现了
尼龙绸、锦丝绸、无纺布和塑料膜
等蒙面材料。

裁：将蒙面材料按照风筝骨架
裁剪出相应的形状。下料时的纸张
要略大于骨架边缘，同时也要考虑
纸的纹理，避免使用倾斜纹理的纸
张，左右纸面纹理要对称。

糊：用乳胶将蒙面材料和骨架
黏合在一起。涂抹乳胶的时候要均
匀，不能太厚。蒙面材料定位黏合

need more than one layer of paper. Some cover the paper with silk and this practice makes a new composite material. Thanks to the advance of science and technology, nylon taffeta, nylon silk, non-woven fabric and plastic film have been used as cover.

Cutting paper of silk: This step is to cut the material into the right size and shape. The material used should be slightly bigger than the size and shape needed. Also, the veins of the material have to be taken into careful

● 校正风筝骨架与蒙面材料（图片提供：全景正片）
Adjust the Structure and the Mounting Material

后用手轻按四周，尽量少移动。

边：修剪多余的蒙面材料，根据风筝大小、黏合强度可分为切边、卷边、缝边和粘边四种方式。切边是当风筝不大、蒙面与骨架黏合度强时，直接用刀切掉多余的蒙面边缘。卷边是当风筝需要增大黏合强度时用剪刀裁下一部分，同时留下一部分蒙面涂胶后卷过来。缝边为风筝需要更大的强度时，在卷边后将多余的部分再缝上。粘边的手法主要是针对塑料膜这类新型材料，由于塑料膜不宜缝合，就要把多余的边缘卷过来再黏合。

校：在蒙面的过程中不断地校正骨架和蒙面的位置，以免骨架扭曲。

consideration. Paper with slanting veins should be avoided and the veins on both sides should be symmetrical.

Pasting: This is to paste the structure with the covering material. Glue should be applied evenly, not to be too thick. After gluing, use fingers to push the mounting material gently to make it firm, not to move it before it is dried up.

Edging: This is to cut off the extra areas on edge by the size of the kite being made. Edging may happen in different ways, cutting, rolling, sewing and pasting. Cutting is simple, and if the size is not too big, simply uses a knife to do it. Rolling is to glue extra parts purposely left to increase strength. Sewing is for more strength by stitches on the glued parts. Pasting is done after rolling about extra of plastic films, which is difficult to be sewed together.

Adjustment: This is to get the exact locations during the process of mounting, to avoid warping that may happen to the structure.

> 风筝的绘制

　　风筝的绘制是一种综合绘画技法的工艺，其在较大程度上决定了风筝的形象和内容。风筝的绘制主要包括色、底、描、染、

> Painting

Painting kites, a process to involve different techniques, decides on the image to appear. Painting involves coloring, foundation application, delineation, dyeing and polishing.

● 绘制风筝的染色颜料
Paints Used for Dyeing

● 风筝艺人哈亦琦在白纸上勾描图案

哈亦琦是著名的北京哈氏风筝的第四代传人，此图为其现场演示风筝的制作。

Ha Yiqi, Kite Maker, Is Working on a Piece of White Paper

Ha Yiqi is the fourth generation of the Ha Family, famous in the trade of kite making in Beijing. He is showing how to paint an image on a piece of white paper for a kite.

修五个方面。

色：中国传统的风筝常用品红、槐黄、品绿和黑色，这四种颜色不仅十分鲜艳，而且相互之间的对比强烈，绘制效果鲜明绚丽。近代透明水色的应用则使得风筝的绘画层次更加丰富。

底：有些风筝在绘画之前需要

Coloring: Traditionally, red, yellow, green and black are much favored because they are bright and they complement one another. In modern times, people use transparent water color to make an image more attractive.

Foundation application: Some kites need foundation color before painting starts. These kites are dragonflies and

上底色，如蜻蜓、金鱼形状的风筝就需先晕染出底色。晕染底色需要在蒙面材料上刷一层水使其湿润，然后再刷上一层透明水色，晾至未完全干时再刷一次，如此反复直到达到要求，待完全干后用熨斗熨平即可。如果没有渐变色的要求，则可用实底上色的方法处理底色。实

goldfish. Use water to make the mounting material wet first before applying a coat of water color. After the material is dried up, repeat the process once again until ideal condition is achieved. Then, iron it until it is completely smooth. If the colors to be used do not graduate in shade, color is applied as a foundation color. This is done by leaving the mounting material

• 风筝图案的染色
Dyeing

底上色是把蒙面材料浸入盛有颜料的平盘中，待全部染色后把染色材料轻拉出来挂置晾干。

描：准备好有底色或无底色的蒙面材料就可以绘画了。画前在白纸上用墨线绘好图案的大样，然后将蒙面材料放在大样上勾描出流畅均匀的线条。

染：为风筝的图案着色。染色

simply in a color plate to pick up the color before taken out to dry up.

Delineation: Then, the delineation on the mounting material either with or without foundation color. Delineation is to draw by ink on white paper the image, then copy it onto the mountain material.

Dyeing: Dyeing is to color, but before that, a coat of vitriol is applied to the mounting material before. After

● **先绘后糊的风筝形态**（图片提供：全景正片）

风筝裱糊和彩绘的顺序一般是先糊后绘，但精细风筝的制作则采用先绘后糊的方式，即先根据设计图纸在蒙面材料上勾线、涂色，再把绘好的蒙面材料准确地糊在风筝骨架上，并进行修饰和调整。

Images Being Painted Before Pasted onto the Structure

Usually, painting an image comes after pasting, but some exquisite kites need to do it reversely, painting on the mounting material first before pasting is done onto the structure for the final touch.

前的蒙面材料上都要上一层矾水，待干后大多选透明水色上色。颜色一次不能上得太浓太厚，浓厚的颜色晾干后表面会僵硬收缩，影响蒙面的使用。

修：染色后对图案、骨架、整体形态的调整。

it is dries up it receives a water color. Water color should not be too thick, or it will make the mounting material hard and shrink after it dries up. If so, it will seriously affect the result.

Polishing: This is the step to do final touches about the images, structure and appearance.

风筝绘制口诀
A Pithy Formula in Rhyme for Painting a Kite

风筝制作的传承一直是口传心授，史料上记载的一些风筝图谱大都没有流传下来。近代发现的曹雪芹《南鹞北鸢考工志》是最早的关于风筝制作的书籍，成为曹氏风筝发展的依据，里面也记载了大量简单易懂的风筝绘制口诀，如：

The skill of kite making has been told by one generation to the next verbally. Many patterns and varieties mentioned in history books have long got lost. *Kite Making in the South and North*, a book authored by Cao Xueqin, is the oldest book about kite making so far discovered, a basis for Cao style kites. It documented many pithy formulas about the skill:

• 小燕风筝
Small Swallow Kite

小燕画诀
Swallow Kite

小燕欲将童子拟，四肢渐大短身躯。

It looks like a toddler, having long limbs and short body.

颈长疑是头颅巨，眉清目秀意顽皮。

It has a long neck, a big head,

lively eyes and graceful eyebrows—looks very naughty.

口角乳黄犹然在，胸中洁白更无欺。

Everything about it is childlike, innocent and honest.

权寄游兴桃园水，且寓逸情武陵溪。

It flies over a garden, or a brook,

尾随蛱蝶觅花圃，时逐鸳鸯戏芙蕖。

It looks down at the flowers below and the love birds in pond.

殷殷祝福椿萱茂，仙寿遐龄过云霄。

Good wishes from it are for everybody and everything,

happiness and longevity.

- 小燕风筝
Small Swallow Kite

> 风筝的放飞

　　制作风筝的最终目的是为了放飞，放飞成功与否体现了风筝是否具有完善的功能。由于风筝的种类繁多，操作方法各不相同，但基本上可以概括为风、线、放、调、收五个方面。

　　风：风筝的飞行需借助空气流动的动力，春秋两季风力适中、风向稳定，是适合放风筝的季节。一般3—4级风力适合中小型风筝，5级风力的天气适合放飞大型硬翅风筝，6级以上的风力最好不放风筝。

　　线：传统的小型风筝宜采用两根提线，中型硬翅风筝的提线多为三根，超大型风筝则需要增加提线数量以保证风筝的刚度。风筝的提线位置由风筝的结构决定，只要在相应的位置绑上提线即可。

> Flying

Flying well or not determines the success of kite making. Different categories have different way to fly, but all involves the following five: wind, thread, flying, adjusting and retrieving.

Wind: All kites need wind to fly. The wind in spring and autumn is moderate and stable in direction. So spring and autumn are the best seasons to fly a kite. The kite to fly depends on the wind force; wind force between three and four are good for small and medium size kites, while wind force five is good for large and hard-wing kites. If the wind force exceeds six, go home.

Thread: Traditional small kites use two threads, while medium-size and hard-wing kites use three, and if the kite is big or super large, more threads for control. The places the threads are attached depend on the structure of kites,

- 中国画《儿童放鹞图》（清）

  Children Flying Kites, Traditional
  Chinese Painting (Qing Dynasty)

风筝的提线可以是尼龙线、钓鱼线、编织线，或者一些光滑耐磨的风筝专用线。

放：风筝放飞需要根据场地的风力情况使用一定的技巧。在风力较弱的情况下，需要助跑一段距离以给予风筝一定的加力。如果场地不够，则需要经常快速向后撤线。风筝升力加重应及时放线，风筝升

simply tied up to these places and it is done. The threads may be nylon, fishing lines or threads for weaving, so long they are smooth and strong.

Flying: It takes skills to make a kite take off. When the wind force is small, one has to run for a distance. If the ground is not large enough, one has to pull or release the thread fast. When the kite is gaining altitude, the threads

• 在草地上助跑以放飞风筝
（图片提供：全景正片）

Take a Run-up on the
Grass to Fly a Kite

● 调整风筝线让风筝飞得更高 （图片提供：微图）

Adjust the Threads for the Kite to Fly Higher

力减弱时要及时收线，通过放线和收线的交替运用让风筝在空中飘飞而不坠落。

调：风筝放飞的过程中，由于不同高度的气流速度不同，需要及时通过风筝线调整风筝的角度、力度来保持风筝飞行的平稳。如风筝的方向出现偏移时，可以细微地移动风筝上的提线；风筝扎根头时，可以将风筝的尾部加重或缩短风筝的提线；而风筝飞不高时，可减轻

need to be released timely and when the wind force is weakening, rewind the threads. By these, a kite is able to stay in the air.

Adjustment: Due to different air flows one needs to adjust the angle and force given to the threads. If the kite is away from the right direction, one may lift the thread attached to the head of the kite, and if the kite is tumbling, pull in the thread attached to the tail to make it heavy. When the kite is low

尾部的重量。

　　收：收回风筝线比较容易，只要注意收线不要太急和避开树木就可以。

in the air, one may reduce the force applied to the tail.

　　Retrieving: Rewind the thread for retrieving is fairly easy, so long one does it with care and avoids trees.

风筝放飞的影响因素

　　任何物体要飞上天空，首先要克服地心引力的影响。风筝只有具备了大于自身重量的升力才可以起飞，这种升力就是空气流动产生的动力。风筝的升空是在放飞时，流过风筝的空气产生一个向下的力，这种力作用于风筝时便推动风筝向上。风筝放飞过程中的调整提线、变换角度等技巧就是针对不同气流而进行的相应调整。

　　除了拴线位置，风筝的形状对放飞也有很大的影响。同样面积的硬翅风筝与

• 风筝《彩蝶》
民间有放风筝的口诀："提线拴得好，风筝飞得高；提线拴不好，风筝放不起。"
Colorful Butterfly Kite
People say, "Correct place for the threads makes a kite fly higher; incorrect place makes the kite difficult to take off."

拍子风筝同时起飞，硬翅风筝起飞速度要略快一些。因为硬翅风筝的翅翼上有一个弧形的风兜，这种弧形翅翼使前后缘线与相对气流平行时仍能产生升力。这也是北京沙燕容易放飞的原因。同样，翅翼的长宽之比与升力大小也有关系，长宽之比越大，风筝在空气中的阻力就越小，升空更快。

Factors Affecting the Kites' Flying

Anything that wants to fly needs to overcome the earth gravity. So long the kite gains lift bigger than its own weight, it takes off. This lift is the power from air flows. The kite takes off by a downward force from air. By adjusting threads and the angle of the kite, kite flies and is stable in the air.

Apart from the position the threads are tied to, the shape of a kite determines easiness or difficulty to fly. Hard-wing kites take off and fly faster than flat kites because the hard-wing has an arch on the wing, which hold the air force to create lift. This fact explains why the swallow kites from Beijing is easy to control in the air. Also, the ratio between the length and width of wings makes difference. The bigger the ratio, the air resistance is smaller and taking-off is faster.

- "仕女" 硬翅风筝
  Maids Hard-wing Kite

风筝流派
Kite Styles

　　中国地域广阔，风筝制作与各地的民俗文化结合而产生了多种风筝形态。在长期的发展中，逐渐形成了北京、天津、潍坊、南通四大风筝产地，这四大产地的风筝受当地的民俗、地域环境、扎制艺人的制作手法等各方面的影响，具有鲜明的特点，成为影响全国的风筝流派。而开封、阳江、西藏等地区的风筝迅速发展，成为中国具有代表性的风筝流派。

Vast China has many kite styles and each is closely related to local customs and culture. Over the past centuries, Chinese kites have seen four major making places: Beijing, Tianjin, Weifang and Nantong, all carrying the features of local custom, geological situation and local craftsmanship. Apart from these four, kite making in Kaifeng, Yangjiang and Tibet have also developed fast. Together, they make the major schools of Chinese kite making.

> 北京风筝

　　关于北京风筝的记载自清代才出现，距今有三百多年的历史。清代潘荣陛编撰的《帝京岁时纪胜》载："清明扫墓，倾城男女，纷出四郊，提酌挈盒，轮毂相望，各携纸鸢线轴，祭扫毕，即于坟前施放较胜。"可见当时放飞风筝的风俗。另外，由于明、清两代定都北京，北京聚集了大量的权臣和贵族，宫廷和权贵的需求使北京风筝极尽工巧，形成精致华美的风格。北京风筝品类繁多，曹雪芹所著的《南鹞北鸢考工志》中就记载有四十多种扎法。现存可供考证的是民国初年的《北平风筝谱》，其中收集了两百多种北京风筝，并详细地介绍了北京风筝的制作方法。北京风筝工艺讲究

> Beijing Style

Documentation in history books of Beijing style kites appeared during the Qing Dynasty over 300 years ago. In his book *Notes About Seasonal Events in Beijing*, Pan Rongbi of the Qing Dynasty said the following: "During the Qingming Festival, people of all ages come to suburbs with food. Their horse-drawn carts often parked hub to hub. After mourning the dead, they fly kites in front of a graveyard for a competition." During the Ming and Qing dynasties, Beijing was the capital where the rich and powerful thronged the city. Kite making had a huge market and the skills were advanced, leaving many works of art. By Cao Xueqin, Beijing style kites had over forty ways to make. By *Kites from Beijing*, a book published in early republican years, Beijing style had over

- 肥燕风筝

  北京沙燕风筝以展翅飞翔的燕子为原型，以夸张的手法强调其舒展的双翅和剪形尾翼，形成一种非常优美高雅的"大"字造型图案。此肥燕风筝采用蓝色描绘图案，故称为"蓝锅底"。

  Fat Swallow Kite

  Swallows are the most favored image for Beijing style kites, their image often having exaggerated wings and scissor-like tails. Together, they make a Chinese character meaning "big". If they are painted on a blue background, the kite is commonly called "blue bottom of cooking pot".

扎、糊、绘、放，骨架扎制轻盈牢固，裱糊工艺精致高超，装饰图案构图饱满、色彩绚丽。

北京风筝以沙燕为代表，也称"扎雁儿"。沙燕的外形模拟燕子的形象，在头、脚和两翼进行变形处理。头是燕子头的平面变形，尖嘴圆眼，眼睛上方饰有飞扬的眉

200 varieties. The book detailed their making technology, which featured elaborate structuring, pasting, beautiful painting, flying technique, solid structures and exuberant patterns.

Among the Beijing style varieties, swallow kites make the representative, shaped just like the bird but transformed at head, feet and wings. The head

- ● **瘦沙燕风筝**

  哈氏风筝多为绢制，骨架平实，画工精致，以瘦沙燕最为出色。此件瘦沙燕风筝的外形修长纤细，沙燕的身上还绘有张牙舞爪的龙，呈现出威严的气势。

  Thin Swallow Kite

  Most kites made by the Ha family have silk as mounting material. They are beautifully painted. Among all, the thin swallow ones are the most famous. The swallow kites of this type are narrow and long, some having a fierce-looking dragon painted to emphasize strength.

眼，眉梢上挑，内部还绘有夸张的睫毛。整个头部不仅具有燕子的特点，还被赋予了人的面部表情。

　　北京的沙燕分为肥燕、瘦燕和雏燕等。肥燕丰润饱满，身短翅膀阔，尾部分叉角度大。瘦燕纤细秀美，身子长，且双翅纤细，尾部长而窄，分叉角度小。雏燕的扎制、绘制方式与肥燕近似，但面部绘制得更饱满短胖，接近儿童的面部比例。

becomes flat, the beak, pointed, the eyes, round even having uplifted eyebrows corners. Some went so far as to have them highly exaggerated. The head was swallow's, but given a human facial expression.

This swallow variety also has variations, some thin, others fat, some having broader wings while some, having an exaggerated cut on tails. The thin swallows are slender and graceful, having a long body, narrow wings, long

• 雏燕风筝《九龙百子》　孔令民制

此雏燕风筝的形态可爱，雏燕身上绘百子舞龙图，寓意吉庆。

Nine Dragons with Hundred Descendents, Kite Made by Kong Lingmin

This swallow kite has nine dragons and a hundred descendents painted on its body to mean auspiciousness.

沙燕尺寸多样，结构简练，主骨架只由五根竹条组成，翅膀由上下两根竹条在端部弯曲而形成形状特殊的"膀兜"，这使沙燕在风小时容易起飞，风大时也能在空中保持平稳。在装饰上，人们在沙燕的前胸、膀窝和尾羽等部位绘制蝙蝠、桃子、牡丹、蝴蝶等吉祥图

but narrow tails with a small cut. Baby swallows are made just like the fat swallows, but have a fat face just like that of a plump boy.

Swallow kites have different sizes but all are briefly structured. Their skeleton has only five bamboo slips. The two on the wings are bent to make a pouch to catch wind for easy take-off

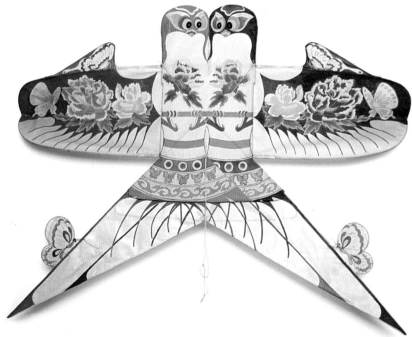

- **比翼燕**

比翼燕由一雌一雄两只燕子组成，燕子的身上绘有富贵牡丹的吉祥图案和前来寻芳的蝴蝶，又构成了一幅美妙的蝶恋花画面。

Double-wing Swallow Kite

A double-wing swallow kite often has two swallows, a male and a female carrying peony or other auspicious patterns. With butterflies coming in, the pattern makes a nice image of happiness.

- 北京硬翅风筝《虎娃献寿》 徐立制

虎被称为山中之王，是驱邪的猛兽之一。此风筝的中心位置为头戴虎帽、顶寿桃的娃娃，四周则布满老虎和蝙蝠的图案，下坠盘长，寓意家中儿童健康富贵。

Baby Tiger Celebrates Father's Birthday, Hardwing Kite, Made by Xu Li

The tiger is taken as the king of animals and able to dispel evil spirits. The central part of this pattern is a baby wearing tiger's hat and holding longevity peach. Around the baby are tigers and bats. This kite has a long pendent below to mean healthy children.

案，以祈求幸福、长寿和富贵。而不同的图案有着不同的寓意，适合不同结构的沙燕。如雏燕两翼绘制荷花，寓意新荷出水、清新纯净；双翼燕上绘制牡丹、蝴蝶组成的蝶恋花图，寓意比翼双飞、白头偕

and balance in the air if wind gets strong. People like to paint auspicious images like bats, peaches, peony and butterflics on the chest, shoulders and tail of a kite as wishes for happiness, fortune and longevity. Different patterns symbolize different needs and suit different kite structures. Lotus painted on wings of a baby swallow stand for purity and innocence, peony and butterflies painted on wings of a pair convey the wish for a happy marriage and a family life that lasts. There is a variation of this type: the double-wing swallows. This variation has two birds, a male and a female who look at each other lovingly. In painting, the double-wing swallows, and single-wing swallow differ. The heads of double-wing swallows incline lovingly to each other to show devotion, showing three fourth of their faces. The single-swallow kite has its head painted square from the front.

From the late Qing Dynasty until present day, Beijing style kites have fallen in four major schools, each represented by Jin Fuzhong, Ha Guoliang,

老。另外，还有一种沙燕的变形品种——比翼燕。比翼燕四目相视，一雌一雄并体而飞，象征夫妻恩爱、家庭幸福。在绘制上，比翼燕与单沙燕略有不同，单沙燕头部是正面，比翼燕取两燕相视的姿态，头部是有透视的四分之三侧面，呈现出两燕相互依偎的样子。

北京风筝从清末流传到现在，比较知名的流派有四个，代表人物分别是金福忠、哈国良、马晋和孔祥泽。金氏风筝兴起于20世纪20年代，创始人金福忠出身于风筝世家，其制作的风筝以"黑沙燕"最为著名，造型粗放，色彩浓烈艳丽，多用对比色来造成强烈的装饰意味。

哈氏风筝在北方享有盛名，风筝骨架坚固平整，材料多为绢制，画工精致，被人们称为"风筝哈"。风筝哈有160年的历史，至今已传至第四代。第二代哈长英不但继承了父亲哈国良的风筝扎制技艺，更汲取其他艺术的特点，制作的风筝颇具特色。而且他还根据各品种的风筝骨架制定出风筝的标准尺寸、样板及造型比例。1915年在

Ma Jin and Kong Xiangze individually. Jin Fuzhong's kites got fame in 1920s. Founder of this school, Jin Fuzhong, came from a kite making family. Among all the kites he made, the black swallows were the best known, having highly decorative bright colors in a pleasant contrast and very boldly painted images.

Kites made by Ha Guoliang were equally famous in the north. The kites he made were strong in structure, neat in appearance and most often, using beautifully painted silk as the mounting material. Because his kites had elaborate silk mounting and beautifully done images, he was affectionately called Kite Ha. Kites of the Ha school are over 160 years old, now managed by the fourth generation of the family. The second generation, Ha Changying, apart inheriting the skills, drew on the benefits from other styles to make his products even more stylistic. For different shapes, he formulated standard size, shape and ratio. His butterfly, dragonfly, phoenix and crane kites won the silver prize in 1915 on the World Expo held in San Francisco. The third and fourth generation of the family made much progress too, on the basis of inheritance.

- 北京硬翅风筝《飞天伎乐》 冷世翔制

  飞天伎乐是佛教中的乐神，能歌善舞，身姿轻盈，常手持乐器飞行于天。此风筝的中间为一位身姿窈窕、挎腰鼓、单脚跳舞的飞天，四周则分布着手拿笛子、琵琶等各种乐器的飞天。

  Flying Apsaras, Hard-wing Kite of Beijing Style, Made by Leng Shixiang

  Flying apsaras is a dancing and singing goddess, gracefully flying in the sky with music instrument in hand. This kite pictures one carrying a waist drum, standing on one leg as if ready to leap. Around her are small apsaras holding musical instruments in hand.

美国旧金山举办的巴拿马国际博览会上，哈长英制作的蝴蝶、蜻蜓、花凤和仙鹤等风筝获得银质奖章和奖状。第三代哈魁明和第四代哈亦琦在继承家传技术的基础上也都各有创新。

马晋原来是画家，其制作的风筝造型规整，设色雅丽，绘制细腻，适合陈设。孔祥泽也是画家出身，以绘见长，因临摹和钻研曹雪芹《南鹞北鸢考工志》而复制出具有特色的"曹氏风筝"。后来，冷世祥、费保龄承袭曹氏风筝，并进行自我创新，丰富了现代北京风筝的形态。

Ma Jin was originally a painting artist. The kites he made were neat in appearance and bright in colors, very nice to work as decorative items. Kong Xiangze had also worked as a painting artist and by reference he found in Cao Xueqin's book, he successfully made the "Cao Family style Kite" characteristic of the southern style. Later, Leng Shixiang and Fei Baoling carried on the Cao family style and innovated; giving Beijing style kites more varieties.

鲁迅与风筝

1925年，中国著名的文学家、思想家、革命家鲁迅先生在北京女子师范大学任教。这一年的1月24日，住在北京的鲁迅看到冬季天空中飘浮的一两只风筝，便触景生情，写出了著名的散文《风筝》。散文一开始，鲁迅即以北京街头所见，向人们展示了一幅冬季放风筝的画面。人们在冬日就急于将风筝放飞到严寒的天空中，使鲁迅不仅惊异于人们对春天的迫切向往，也唤醒了鲁迅心中珍藏的故乡二月放风筝的情景。通过温和春日与寒冷冬日下的风筝的对比，鲁迅以借物言志的艺术手法，表达了对当时并不明朗的时局的担忧，富含深厚的爱国情怀。

Lu Xun and Kites

On January 1925, while Lu Xun, writer, thinker and revolutionary, was teaching in Female High Normal College of Beijing, he was inspired by two kites flying in the sky and wrote one of his most famous essays, *Kite*. He began by picturing an ordinary winter day of Beijing, when someone was anxious to fly a kite into the sky in spite of cold weather. To him, this was the sign of people's longing for the coming spring season. It made him think of his hometown, where people flying kites in the second month of Chinese lunar calendar. By contrast of kites flying in winter and spring, he expressed his worry about the political situation then. The prose makes a fine release of patriotism.

● 鲁迅画像
Portrait of Lu Xun

● 北京永定门城楼放风筝的市民 (图片提供：微图)
People Flying Kites by the Yongding Gate of Beijing

> 天津风筝

天津作为工商业发展较早的城市之一，汇集了全国各地的手工艺人，这直接促进了天津风筝的发展。在清代的杨柳青年画《十美图放风筝》中，即可看到有盘鹰、蝴蝶、奔马等图案的风筝。天津风筝的变革性发展是在清末民初，喜欢风筝的文人开始对风筝进行研究改进，利用丝线代替纸捻来扎接骨架和用翎毛管衔接骨架等，使天津风筝形成品类繁多、工艺精湛的面貌。

天津风筝以软翅风筝为主。软翅结构采用软性的布或绢为裱糊材料，可以使制成的飞鸟或昆虫的翅膀更加轻盈，也可以使神仙人物的衣袖和身边的云彩更加飘逸。软翅风筝在绘制上多采用

> Tianjin Style

As a city of commerce progressing earlier than others, Tianjin had craftsmen coming in from across the country and this boosted its kite making trade. A Yangliuqing New Year painting, *Ten Beauties Flying Kites*, depicts this popular activity there. It has eagle, butterfly, galloping horse kites. The kite making trade of Tianjin can be traced to the late Qing and early Republican years, when scholars turned their eyes to this toy. They did much improvement like replacing paper thread with silk ones, feather tubes as joins for different parts. With the improvements, Tianjin style has many varieties, all elaborately made.

Most Tianjin style kites are soft-wing ones, with either cloth or silk as the mounting material and this made their bird or insect kites lighter, graceful dressing for human or immortal figures and clouds. Soft-wing kites often have warm and cold

• 天津杨柳青年画《十美图放风筝》

此年画描绘了妇女在春天踏青、放风筝的欢快场景，画面上的风筝类别多样，包括串类风筝、蝙蝠风筝、蝴蝶风筝、人物风筝和宫灯风筝等。

Ten Beauties Flying Kites, New Year Painting from Yangliuqing, Tianjin

This painting illustrates how women enjoy themselves by flying kites in spring. The kites they fly are in different varieties, stringed, bats, butterflies, human images and palatial lanterns.

冷暖色对比的着色手法，强烈的色彩对比能够形成绚烂的视觉效果。而飞禽翎羽、昆虫翅膀、鱼类的鳍等则采用晕染手法着色，形象逼真灵动。

软翅风筝最具特色的是骨架扎制结构，骨架结构采用扣楔、

colors in a sharp contrast for a strong visual impact, while birds, insects, and fish fins are shady colored for vividness.

The most striking feature about soft-wing kites is their structure, joined not by threads, but by buckles of different kinds. This feature enabled their kites lighter and easier to carry along. Also, these

拆折和盔头的方式，装置奇巧。
在扎制风筝骨架时不用线绑而使
用扣楔相接，可以使风筝折叠自
如，便于携带，即使是很大的风
筝也能拆开放进很小的盒子里。
同时，扣楔结构还便于安置特技
装置，增加放飞乐趣。盔头则是
用棉纸在模子里粘成薄壳，做成
各种风筝的头部。这种方式可以

buckle joints allow a big kite to be carried
into a small box after disassembling.
And there is more: it is able to carry a
special installation for more amusement.
Kite heads are shells made with molded
cotton paper, no longer limited by the
mounting material. They can be made in
three dimensions, lighter, more vivid and
impressive.

Another feature of Tianjin style kites

• 天津软翅风筝《子孙万代》 周树
堂制

此风筝为多层软翅风筝，色彩艳
丽，有极强的装饰性。风筝上的葫
芦有多子的寓意，蝴蝶象征富贵长
寿。

Prosperous Descendents, Tianjin-
style Soft-wing Kite, Made by Zhou
Shutang

This soft-wing kite has multiple wings
in bright colors, very decorative. The
gourd seeds painted symbolize many
descendents, and the five butterflies
painted around the gourd mean wealth
and longevity.

使风筝不受扎架糊纸的局限，重量既轻，外形又美，而且立体形态的头部显得更加逼真。

天津风筝的另一特色是团组类型的风筝，即将数量众多的小风筝排列在一起组成一个大风筝。如用数只蝴蝶围绕着葫芦而组成的"子孙万代"风筝，软翅制作的蝴蝶簇拥着装饰华美的葫芦，放至空中时蝴蝶翅膀随风飘动，别具特色。还有一种名为"百鸟朝凤"的风筝，由各种鸟雀围绕着凤凰组成。

天津风筝也善于安装精巧的装置。最独特的是天津风筝名手魏元泰制作的蒲绷风筝和锣鼓燕风筝。蒲绷是一种芦苇，蒲绷风筝要采用特定季节的蒲绷来扎，将蒲绷拴在用细藤条弯曲成的小弓上，再挂绑在风筝上，放飞时就能发出近似筝鸣的声音。如果将风筝的线拴在柱子上，风筝可一夜不落、声响不停，声音可传500米远。锣鼓燕是挂着小锣鼓和小风车装置的风筝，放飞时锣鼓作响。

天津风筝以魏元泰的作品为最佳，其风格清新明快、色彩绚丽、骨架轻盈。魏元泰被称为"风筝

is their composition, many small kites grouped together to make a big one, like "prosperous descendents" kite, which has gourds, each having several butterflies around. In the sky, these gourds give a pleasant sound and the wings of butterflies flap. Another representative kite of Tianjin style is "hundred birds paying respect to phoenix". Birds of different kinds are surrounding a phoenix.

Tianjin style kites may also have elaborate gadgets on them, but the best known kind was made by Wei Yuantai, seen in his reed kites and "gonging and drumming swallow" kites. The reed kites used only seasonal reed, bent and attached to a bow like thing before attached to the kite. In the air, this kind of kites gave a musical sound. If you tied a type of this kind to a place, the kite would stay in the air and gave the sound all night, audible within five hundred meters around. The "gonging and drumming" swallow kites had, as their name suggested, small gongs and drums. In the air, they gave a mixture of gonging and drumming.

The best known kite maker in Tianjin was Wei Yuantai. The kites he made were bright in color and light in weight. He was affectionately called "Kite Wei". His skill has been handed down to

• 天津风筝《八仙庆寿》 魏元泰制

此风筝以传统的八仙为题材，八仙脚踏云彩环绕在大红的"寿"字旁边，画面协调美观，并以重彩勾勒的艺术手法追求浓厚的装饰趣味。

Eight Immortals at Birthday Party, Tianjin-style Kite, Made by Wei Yuantai

This kite has the eight immortals in clouds, very symmetrically arranged around the character "longevity", and delineated with heavy color for a decorative purpose.

• **天津风筝《丹凤朝阳 》 魏元泰制**

丹凤朝阳是中国传统的吉祥图案之一，寓意贤才遇良机，有完美、吉祥、前途光明的含义。

Magic Birds Facing the Sun, Tianjin-style Kite, Made by Wei Yuantai

This is a traditional pattern meaning good opportunities, perfection, auspiciousness and bright future.

• "风筝魏"第三代传人魏永昌夫妇（图片提供：FOTOE）
The Couple of Wei Yongchang, the Third Generation of Kite Wei

魏"，至今已传至第四代。魏元泰对天津风筝制作技术的变革作出了重大贡献，研制出平拍类、圆形立体类、软翅和折翅风筝。魏元泰不仅革新风筝种类，还注重吸取其他艺术的精华，使其制作的风筝富于装饰美感。清朝末年，慈禧太后曾派人到天津向魏元泰定做风筝，溥仪皇帝在天津居住时也曾派人购"魏记"风筝，曾任中华民国大总统的黎元洪则亲自购买过他的风筝。

his fourth generation. Wei Yuantai did much improvement on kite making. He developed different varieties, soft-wing, hard wing, round, three dimensional, and of course, flat ones. By drawing on the benefits of other forms of art, the kites Wei Yuantai made were highly beautiful, highly decorative. Among his customers were the Empress Dowager Cixi, the last emperor of the Qing Dynasty Puyi while he was staying in Tianjin and the President of the Republican Li Yuanhong.

> 潍坊风筝

潍坊位于山东半岛中部，是风筝的发祥地，也是闻名的"世界风筝之都"。潍坊风筝自宋代开始流行，至明代更加普及，到清代时已在全国十分盛行。据记载，清代潍坊城里的风筝作坊和店铺就有三十余家，商家所售风筝品种众多、粗细皆全。如今，潍坊更是以风筝誉满中外。潍坊风筝选材讲究、扎制骨架外形优美、裱糊工艺精巧、绘制色彩艳丽、起飞灵活。风筝已经成为潍坊的代名词。

潍坊风筝在发展过程中吸收了该地区其他艺术门类的特点，发展出具有鲜明地方特色的艺术风格，逐渐形成了潍坊杨家埠风筝和潍县风筝两大流派。潍坊杨家埠风筝与杨家埠年画结合紧密，是杨家埠

> Weifang Style

Weifang in the central part of the Shandong Peninsula is the birthplace of kites. It is described as "the capital of kites of the world". Kite making in Weifang began during the Song Dynasty, popular during the Ming Dynasty and spread to other parts of the country during the Qing Dynasty, when Weifang had over 30 established family businesses and shops. The kites they made were in many varieties and sizes. Weifang kites feature fine selection of materials, beautiful structure, nice mounting and gorgeous painting. They are easy to fly. Weifang is forever mentioned with kite-making.

Weifang style kites have borrowed features of others before they progressed into current two major genres: Yangjiabu and Weixian. Yangjiabu kites are closely related to the Yangjiabu style New Year paintings, made by woodblock artists in

● 潍坊杨家埠风筝《蝴蝶》

Butterfly, Yangjiabu Style Kite, Weifang

版画艺人在闲暇时制作出来的。杨家埠年画是中国年画的主要产地之一，风格多样，或工细缜密，或简括秀丽，或线条流畅。杨家埠风筝的题材多以年画题材为主，涉及鸟兽植物、器物陈设、神话传说、历史人物，以及福禄寿、五子登科、麒麟送子等吉祥图案。另外，风筝图案的绘制采用版画印制和绘制结

their spare time. Yangjiabu is a major New Year painting making place in China. Its style features flowing lines in delicate delineation. Most popular subject matter includes flowers, birds, figures from history, legendary animals, characters from folktales and auspicious traditional patterns. These images also appear on kites by painting and wood block artists. As a sister art form to New

合的手法，不仅具有鲜明的杨家埠版画特征，而且节省了绘制时间和成本。潍县风筝由于有彩扎艺人和文人参与制作，所以扎制讲究、风格细腻传神，绘制上较杨家埠风筝更为精致。

作为潍坊风筝的两大流派，潍县风筝和杨家埠风筝主要有三种基本造型，即串式风筝、硬翅风筝和

Year Painting, these images reduce the cost in time and money. The Weixian genre, because mounting artists and men of letters were involved, looked more exquisite than Yangjiabu genre.

Put together, the two genres had three basic forms: the stringed, geometric and hard-winged. Of the three, the large stringed one is most characteristic. From this form developed large centipedes

● 潍坊风筝《龙头蜈蚣》

龙头蜈蚣是潍坊风筝的代表，尤其是龙头的扎制极有特色。

Centipede with Dragon's Head, Weifang Style Kite

Dragon-head centipede kites make the representative of Weifang style. The making technique of its dragon head is highly featuring.

● 潍坊杨家埠软翅风筝
Soft-wing Kite of Yangjiabu Style, Weifang

几何形风筝。其中以大型长串的蜈蚣风筝最为特别，并逐渐演变出以龙头替代蜈蚣头的龙头蜈蚣风筝，成为潍坊风筝的代表作。蜈蚣风筝的尺寸可大可小，小的可放在掌上，大的有几百米长。如1984年4

and still further, centipedes with dragon heads. This image has become the logo of Weifang kites. The size of centipede kites may be large or small. The smallest may be as big as a palm size while the biggest, several hundred meters long. In April 1984, a gigantic centipede with a dragon

月在潍坊的北海滩上就放起了一条巨型龙头蜈蚣风筝，其头高4米、长4米，腰节直径1.2米，全身共长320米。蜈蚣风筝的造型、色彩也各不相同，既有白纸为身、红纸为头、不置一笔、不着一色的蜈蚣风筝，也有色彩缤纷、绘制艳丽的九头神龙风筝。另外，巨型蜈蚣风筝的放飞也不同于普通风筝的放飞，要先把尾部的小风筝放起，然后逐渐放飞大的长串风筝，并带动龙头

head, 4 meters tall and four meters long for its dragon head, 1.2 meters wide on each section and 320 meters long put together, appeared on a beach in Weifang. Dragon-headed centipede kites are made in different colors and shapes, some having white body and red head, some having no brushstroke or color left on its body. Some are gorgeously painted with a nine-head dragon. Gigantic kites have a different way to fly. The smaller kites on its tails fly first to pull up the

• 潍坊风筝《仙鹤童子》

此风筝的造型为一个身穿五彩衣服的童子骑鹤而来，鹤含寿桃两枚，寓意长寿。

Crane and Boy, Weifang Style Kite

This kite has a boy in colorful coat on a crane back, which holds two peaches on its beak to symbolize longevity.

起飞。

潍坊风筝在长期发展中形成了风筝世家和多位风筝制作名家，有"风筝十二名家"之说。陈哑巴和王福斋是清代最为著名的风筝艺人，王福斋的风筝作品《仙鹤童子》和《雷震子背文王》流传至今。

body, then the head.

The Weifang style kites had many established makers. People say it had 12 most famous ones. Chen Yaba and Wang Fuzhai stood out of others during the Qing Dynasty. *Crane and Boy* and *Warrior Lei Zhenzi Carrying on His back Ruler Wen* , two patterns developed by Wang Fuzhai, are still made today.

• 潍坊风筝《喜鹊报喜》

喜鹊是吉祥幸运之鸟，喜鹊报喜预示着喜事到来和幸福如意。此风筝两翼上的喜鹊立在花枝上，两尾上的喜鹊则展翅向花枝飞去，喜鹊形象多变。

Magpie Delivering Happy Message, Weifang Style Kite

This is a pattern to announce the arrival of happiness. Two magpies stand on the tips of wings while the magpies on tails are flying to flowers. Magpies for this style of kites may take different forms.

- 潍坊风筝《张果老倒骑驴》

  此风筝是典型的蘑菇伞风筝，整体形象为插着荷花、绿叶的花瓶，花瓶上绘着张果老倒骑驴的图案。张果老是八仙之一，常倒骑能日行万里的驴，手里则拿着装了两根铁棍的竹筒作为打击乐器。

  Zhang Guolao on Donkey Back in a Reversed Way, Weifang Style Kite

  It is a mushroom shape, resembling a vase with lotus flower and green leaves. On the "vase" is painted the image of Zhang Guolao on donkey back. Zhang Guolao is one of the eight immortals, able to cover several thousand kilometer distance a day. The two iron rods he has are his weapon, also his percussion musical instrument.

潍坊国际风筝节

　　潍坊国际风筝节于每年4月20日至25日举行，有来自30多个国家和地区的代表团参赛。活动内容包括开幕式与放飞仪式、国际风筝比赛、评选世界风筝十绝、参观潍坊风筝博物馆、观看杨家埠民间艺术表演等。自1984年以来，潍坊国际风筝节迄今已连续举办30届，吸引着大批中外风筝专家和爱好者的观赏、竞技和游览。1988年4月1日，第5届潍坊国际风筝会召开主席团会议，与会代表一致通过确定潍坊市为"世界风筝都"的决定。1989年第六届潍坊国际风筝会期间，成立了由中国、美国、日本、英国、意大利等16个国家和地区风筝组织参加的"国际风筝联合会"，并决定把总部设在潍坊。

Weifang International Kite Festival

This annual festival is held between April 20 and 25, participated by over 30 countries and areas. The festival includes opening and flying ceremonies and a competition, selection of the ten best

● 中国杨家埠民间艺术大观园
China Yangjiabu Folk Art Museum, Weifang, China

kites across the world and visits by participants to local kite museum and the show of Yangjiabu folk art show. Beginning from 1984, this festival has been held over 30 cessions, each drawing a large group of Chinese and foreign kite lovers. On April 1, 1988, on the meeting by the presidium of the fifth festival, Weifang was made "the capital of kite making in the world". On the sixth session of the festival, the International Kites Association was founded with organizations from 16 countries including China, U.S. Britain, Japan and Italy, which decided to make Weifang its headquarters.

● 杨家埠风筝博物馆
Yangjiabu Kite Museum

> 开封风筝

开封位于河南省东部，古称"汴梁"、"东京"、"汴京"，是中国八大古都之一。开封风筝历史悠久，在每年农历正月至三月的庙会上，人们竞相放飞各式各样的风筝，场面十分壮观。

开封风筝种类繁多，有软翅类风筝、硬翅类风筝和微型风筝等。开封的软翅类风筝多以蜻蜓、蝴蝶、蜈蚣、仙鹤、鹰等飞禽走兽为题材，形象十分生动；硬翅类风筝色彩浓丽，图案以太极图、七星和大脚燕较为常见，造型夸张而搭配合理；微型风筝可放于掌上，小巧精致，不仅可以放飞，而且可用于收藏。在这些风筝中，以"巨龙风筝"最有名气。巨龙风筝是长200余米、头部重约20千克的大型风筝，

> Kaifeng Style

Kaifeng in the eastern part of Henan Province, one of the eight capital cities in ancient China, had different names in history. Its kite making has a long history. On the temple fair between the first and the third month of lunar calendar, many people fly kites making a splendid scene.

Kaifeng style kites have different varieties, soft-winged, hard-winged and mini. The soft-winged kites may be vividly painted butterfly, dragonfly, centipede, crane and eagle, while the hard-winged kites may have Tai Chi, the seven stars or big-feet swallow images. All are boldly imaged and exaggerated. Mini kites are about the palm size. They can fly and also make nice collectables. But the most famous is gigantic dragon, about 200 meters long and its head, 20 kilos in weight. In the sky, it looks just like a flying dragon.

- 开封龙亭公园里的风筝表演（图片提供：FOTOE）
图为2006年4月12日龙亭公园风筝艺术节上的巨龙风筝。
Kite Flying Performance Inside the Longting Park, Kaifeng
This is the gigantic dragon kite shown on the Longting Kite Festival held on April 12, 2006.

放飞后如一条巨龙在半空中翱翔，气势磅礴。

　　开封风筝的繁荣与众多风筝艺人有密切的关系，这些用料考究、制作精细的风筝艺人促使风筝制作成为开封的一个专门行业。开封的风筝艺人主要分为两种类型：一类是制作传统风筝的艺人，他们的风筝作品具有典型的民间风格和浓厚的乡土气息。另一类是制作竞技风筝的艺人，他们扎制的风筝大多用于比赛。

The prosperity of kite making in Kaifeng was closely related to its large number of kite makers with the best material and superlative skills. They made kite-making a special trade. They fell in two kinds, one being those who made traditional kites and their products showed a strong local feature; the other kind are those who made kites for competition, making flying kites a competitive sport.

• 开封风筝《彩蝶》
Colorful Butterfly, Kaifeng Style Kite

> 南通风筝

南通位于江苏省东南部，东抵黄海，南望长江，是中国著名的风筝产地之一。南通风筝以放飞时的独特音响效果著称，与北方的造型风筝形成鲜明的对比，特别是板鹞和活鹞风筝具有浓郁的地域特色。

板鹞为平板风筝，用细竹竿和布扎制而成，一般长2—3米，大的有4米。板鹞外形简洁古朴，有正方形、长方形、六角形、八角形等，其中以六角、八角板鹞最有特色。六角板鹞是由一个长方形与一个正方形组合成的带有六个凸角的风筝，八角板鹞就是以两个正方形组合而成、带有八个凸角的风筝。而以六角风筝为基础结构，多个六角风筝连接起来就组成了"连星风筝"，如"七连星"、"九连星"

> Nantong Style

Nantong by the sea in southeastern part of Jiangsu Province has the Yangtze River to its south. It is one of the major kite making places in China. Nantong style kites feature with an agreeable sound they give in the air. Also, they are different from the kites made in the north. Snipe birds there are very special.

These birds kites are flat in square, rectangular, hexagon or octagon but the last two are the most commonly seen. The hexagon ones are made up with a rectangular or a square shape with six protruding corners, while the octagon ones have two square shapes with eight. More hexagon ones, when stringed, make multiple-star kites of seven, nine, even up to 61.

These snipe bird kites often take characters from history, a folk tale or an auspicious pattern as the theme, some

风筝，甚至有多达"六十一连星"的风筝。

板鹞的题材以神话传说、历史故事、吉祥图案和宗教信仰为主，图案多出自当地彩扎艺人之手，绘制形象逼真，多采用工笔重彩的技法，红、黑、青、紫等色对比强烈。板鹞的特色是上面装置有数十只乃至数百只大小不一的哨子。哨子材料十分考究，有栗壳、桂圆壳、白果壳、鹅毛管、葫芦、竹子、蚕壳等材质，一般以葫芦哨和

being religious. Painting is usually done by local mounting artists done in red, black, green and purple in sharp contrast. *Ban jiu*, or flat snipe bird kites, may carry tens, even a hundred whistles in different sizes. These whistles are finely made with the shells of chestnuts, longan and ginkgo, or goose quill, wood or bamboo or silkworm shells but mostly of gourd or bamboo. Because of their different sizes, the sound they give are in different tones. These kites are big, and plus the sound devices, they are much heavier

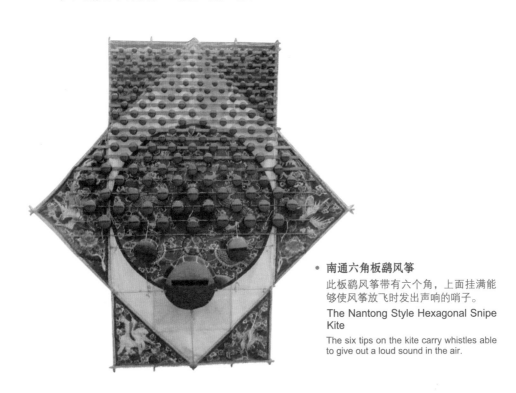

• 南通六角板鹞风筝

此板鹞风筝带有六个角，上面挂满能够使风筝放飞时发出声响的哨子。

The Nantong Style Hexagonal Snipe Kite

The six tips on the kite carry whistles able to give out a loud sound in the air.

● **南通七连星板鹞风筝**

此板鹞风筝由七个六角板鹞风筝连接而成，整体看上去像是一个张开手臂的人物形状。此风筝图案丰富，包括人物、花卉、蝴蝶和神兽等。

The Seven-star Snipe Kite of Nantong Style

This kite has seven hexagonal kites strung together. They resemble a man extending his arms. Decorative patterns may be human figures, flowers, butterflies and legendary animals.

竹哨为多。由于哨子大小不一，发出的声响也分高音部与低音部。板鹞自身体积巨大，加上装载了声响组件，其重量较普通风筝大了许多，如一只2.6米长的板鹞风筝的总重量有9千克左右，这就决定了风力需要达到5级以上才能够顺利

than ordinary kites. A 2.6 meter long bird kite may weigh 9 kilos and need wind force up to five grade to take off and give a sound. Wind in a coastal area often has big winds. Local favorable elements make this kind of birds possible.

Another kind of bird kite, *huo yao*, is also popular, often seen in the shape

放飞和达到放飞后的声响效果。地处海滨的南通常年吹刮海风，这优越的自然条件使板鹞风筝在此产生和发展。

活鹞风筝是南通另一种著名的风筝，造型十分出众，常见的有鹰、燕、蜈蚣、蝴蝶、金鱼、仙佛、美人等。南通活鹞风筝以如皋

of eagle, swallow, centipede, butterfly, goldfish, woman or Buddhist images. This kind has many appearances, but the most famous comes from Rugao, made in different varieties, all being lively and faithfully by local craftsmen. Fine examples are 9-swallow, even 13-swallow kites. Not only unique in design, is this kind also different in the

风筝

● 飘荡在南通广场上的风筝（图片提供：微图）
Kite Floating in the Square of Nantong

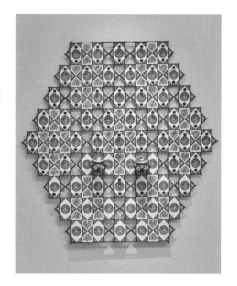

• 南通六十一连星板鹞风筝 郭承毅制
此板鹞风筝由61个六角板鹞风筝连接而成，形成上下、左右均对称的梯形形状的风筝。

Nantong Style 61-star Snipe Kite, Made by Guo Chengyi

This kite has 61 hexagonal kites strung together from side to side, from up to below in a ladder shape.

所出最为有名，式样众多，无巧不具。其造型多出自彩扎艺人之手。在骨架扎制上，吸收了民间灯彩的扎制技艺，篾细骨轻，结构精巧；绘制上，色彩明快，画工精致，形象逼真。如经典的一排九雁、十三雁阵风筝，布阵合理，独具特色。如皋的活鹞风筝不仅奇巧，而且放飞技术也有特色。清末民初的风筝名家石紫寿扎制的老鹰风筝，只要在鹰嘴上牵一根绳子便能上天盘旋，形态惟妙惟肖。近代如皋的风筝以郭氏风筝为代表，郭氏风筝在自身风筝特点的基础上，对《南鹞北鸢考工志》中记载的风筝进行了复制和改进。

way of flying. Just one thread attached to the beak of the eagle kite Shi Zishou made was able to make it hover in the air. The kites made by the Guo family in Rugao, based on their own benefits, showed improvements on traditional ones documented in the book *Kite Making in the South and North*.

> 阳江风筝

阳江地处广东西南沿海，紧邻珠江三角洲，所产风筝是广东风筝的代表。阳江风筝种类繁多，造型结构以简洁见长，基本是两翼一竿一弓，翼宽33厘米，竿长100厘米，弓长66厘米。蒙在风筝骨架上的多是一种含棉料较多的白楚纸，弓弦材质为竹根片或薄铜片。风筝题材除常见的花鸟、走兽、鱼虫、人物等，还有当地特有的墨鱼、对虾。阳江风筝多在秋天放飞，且放飞形态好。其中，最有代表性的是龙头蜈蚣风筝、灵芝风筝和花草鹞风筝。

阳江出产的龙头蜈蚣风筝造型古朴，别具特色。在蜈蚣的形体设计上使用带有草根的茎当做横杆，横杆两侧没有装饰。在每一段腰

> Yangjiang Style

Kites made in Yangjiang in southwest Guangdong next to the Pearl River Delta represent the kite making in Guangdong Province. Yangjiang style kites are in different varieties, mostly in a long shape briefly structured, double-winged with a rod and a bow. Their wings might be 33 cm in width and 100 cm in length. Its bow might be 66 cm long. Most of its mounting material is white cotton paper. The bow string uses bamboo slips or very thin copper film. Decorative patterns are often flowers and birds, fish and insects, and local produces like cuttlefish and shrimp. Flying kite often happens in autumn, when natural conditions are favorable. The most representative are centipede with dragon head, lucid ganoderma (*Lingzhi*), flower or other kinds of vegetation.

● 广东放飞风筝的图景（清）
Kite Flying in Guangdong (Qing Dynasty)

节下都附有一条纸舌，放飞时随风
而动，模仿蜈蚣百足的形态。蜈蚣
风筝长可达百米，放至空中神态逼
真，有些附加特殊装置，在放飞时
通过风筝线操控可实现龙吐珠、戏
鞭炮、龙头吐火等特效。

灵芝风筝是阳江最有特色的风

The dragon-head centipede kites
made in Yangjiang are very special.
They use grass root as supporting rod
without decoration on either side. The
grass root serves as a damper to increase
air resistance. Below each section of
the centipede is a slip of paper which
flickers in wind to imitate the feet of the

阳江灵芝风筝

Lingzhi Kite, Made in Yangjiang

centipede when moving. Such a kite may be a hundred meters long, very much resembling in air. Some has installations able to "spit out a pearl", set off firecrackers, even spit fire from mouth.

Lingzhi kites are the most characteristic of Yangjiang. They are often in a fan shape with an oval "cloud" on tip, taking up half of the space, on which are painted birds, animals, flowers or a plot from a tale. Below the cloud is a big *lingzhi* plant, carried along by a running deer. The most special about this kind of kites is the sound device placed on the tip, made with an oiled thin slice of cane, able to give off a very resounding sound in the air. Its decorative patterns are also diversified, like lotus leaves or figures from traditional story White Snake. In 1990, this kite was made "one of the ten best kites in the world" on the Seventh

筝之一。灵芝风筝整体呈扇形，顶端是一椭圆形的白云，约占整个中骨的二分之一。白云上绘制鸟兽花卉、人物故事等题材；白云下是一株硕大的灵芝草，灵芝草底端被一只奔跑着的小鹿衔着。灵芝风筝的特别之处在于风筝顶端的声响装置，即在风筝的顶端弓架上有一根涂上油的张开的薄藤片，放飞时风吹弦响，声音清亮。1990年，在第七届国际风筝会上，灵芝风筝《白蛇》被评为"世界十绝风筝"之一。

阳江风筝中传播最为广泛的是被称为花草鹞的风筝。这类风筝扎制简单，题材广泛，多与广东地区的民俗紧密结合。

International Kite Festival.

The most commonly seen kites of Yangjiang style are flower and grass kites, simple to make and diversified in subject matter, but often closely related to local customs.

● **阳江龙头风筝**
此龙头风筝的身体由当地特有的带根茅草制成，古朴有趣。
Dragon-head Kite Made in Yangjiang
The body of this dragon-head kite is made with local weed with root, looking very ancient and humorous.

> 西藏风筝

　　西藏自治区的各个地区都有放风筝的习俗，在拉萨和日喀则的城镇中尤为集中。风和日丽之时，男女老少均会加入到放风筝的娱乐活动中，场面壮观而又热闹。

　　西藏风筝的形态以几何形为主，结构大都十分简洁。几何形风筝的制作方法是将一张纸裁成所需的几何形状，并用两根削好的竹条做轴。中轴通过几何形的中心，垂直贴在纸张上成为风筝的头尾；横轴的两端则弯曲成一把拉满弦的弓，安置在两翅的顶角。制成的风筝形体、大小不一，骨架上的轴也有粗细的差别，风大时适合用粗轴，风小时适宜用细轴。西藏风筝上的图案虽然较为简单，但寓意深刻。如在风筝上端用红色或黑

> Tibetan Style

People in every part of Tibet like to fly kites, particularly in Lhasa and Shigatse. Flying kite is seen in every sunny day by people of all ages. It is a very spectacular scene.

　　Tibetan kites are often briefly made in geometrical shapes. Paper is cut into the needed shape. Two bamboo sticks, after being cut, serve as the axles. The central axle is pasted at the center to make the kite's head and tail. Its both ends are bent into bows in full to make the tips of the wing. Tibetan kites may be big or small, and the bamboo sticks used, thin or thick needed. When the wind is big, the thick axle is used. When the wind is small, the thin axle is used. Their decorative patterns, though brief, carry much cultural message. The triangular shape in either red or back stands for the head of Dhamapala. The hook-like

- **西藏风筝** （图片提供：FOTOE）
Tibetan Kite

色画出三角形的形状，表示护法神
的头部；在风筝的两侧画上钩形图
案，则代表恐怖的魔鬼；在风筝上
用各种颜色画出彩色的条纹，象征
着姑娘漂亮的装饰品；在风筝上用
红色或黑色画上宽的条纹，表示法
力无限。

　　西藏风筝放飞时要求的技巧性
较强，放风筝的人需通过放线和收
线使风筝在空中迅速升降、旋转或
翻滚，有的也会在风筝尾部加一条

patterns on either side mean devils, while
color stripes stand for the ornaments
girls wear. The red or black wide strips
symbolize the invincible power of
Buddhist gods.

　　It takes skills to fly a Tibetan
kite. One has to manipulate the thread
skillfully to make the kite ascend or
descend, whirl or roll. Some kites have
a long tail for balance. The thread roller
may be made in six, eight or even ten
axles shape for different age groups of

● 西藏风光
西藏位于中国的西南边陲，地域辽阔，地貌壮观。
Spectacular View in Tibet
Tibet in China's southwest is vast with spectacular geological features.

尾巴来控制平衡。放飞时用于卷线的轴轮结构分为六轴型、八轴型和十轴型，分别适用于不同年龄段的放飞者。另外，风筝线质量的好坏也影响着放飞的结果，人们一般会在线上涂抹耐磨浆。耐磨浆的主要成分有植物的粘胶、面粉、糖料、水等，将这些原料按比例放到锅里煮开，待冷却后就要涂抹到风筝线上，可使风筝线结实耐用。

people. The quality of the thread has much to do with the flying. Usually, the thread has a coat of wear-resistance paste, which is often made with glue, wheat flour, sugar and water in a set ratio after being boiled and applied when it is cool. This will make the thread much tougher.

《中国红》出版编辑委员会

主　任	王亚非
副 主 任	田海明　林清发
编　委	（以姓氏笔划为序）

　　　　　　王亚非　毛白鸽　田海明　包云鸠

　　　　孙建君　任耕耘　吕军　吕品田

　　　　吴鹏　杜国新　林清发　赵国华

　　　　　徐雯　涂卫中　唐元明　韩进

　蒋一谈

执行编委　　任耕耘　蒋一谈

中国红系列

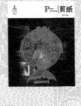

传统手工艺
Traditional Handicraft

中国色彩
Chinese Colors

刺绣
Embroidery

中国禅
Chinese Zen Buddhism

中国棋艺
Art of Chinese Board Games

宋词
Ci-poems of the Song Dynasty

茶马古道
Ancient Tea-Horse Road

中国名湖
Famous Lakes in China

中国料器
Chinese Glassware

帝王陵寝
Royal Mausoleums in China

中华传统美德
Traditional Virtues of China

中国姓氏
Chinese Surnames

传统家具
Traditional Chinese Furniture

中国名山
Famous Mountains in China

中国染织
Chinese Dyeing and Weaving

武术
Chinese Martial Arts

民间玩具
Folk Toys

中国古代教育
Education in Ancient China

中国神话传说
Chinese Mythology and Legends

中国传统游戏
Chinese Traditional Games

四大名著
China's Four Great Classic Novels

中国古代科学
Science in Ancient China

金银器
Gold and Silver Articles

竹木牙角器
Art Crafts Made of Bamboo, Wood, Ivory and Horn

风筝
Kites

中国盆景
Chinese Bonsai

景泰蓝
Cloisonné

泥塑
Clay Sculpture

面塑
Dough Modeling

大运河
The Grand Canal

中国历史名城
Historical and Famous Cities in China

中国结
Chinese Knot

秦陵与兵马俑
The Mausoleum of Qin Shi Huang and Terracotta Warriors

皮影
Shadow Play

古代帝王
Ancient Emperors

中国陶器
Chinese Pottery

中国漆器
Chinese Lacquerware

中国名寺
Famous Temples in China

中国石窟
Chinese Grottoes

中国古桥
Chinese Ancient Bridges

中国名塔
Famous Pagodas in China

中国民居
Chinese Civil Residents

民间戏曲
Chinese Folk Opera

中国灯彩
Chinese Lanterns

诸子百家
The Hundred Schools of Thought

中国牌坊
Chinese Memorial Archways

中国茶艺
Tea Art in China

秦砖汉瓦
Qin Bricks and Han Tiles

面具
Masks

颐和园
The Summer Palace

鼻烟壶
Snuff Bottle

丝绸之路
The Silk Road

汉字
Chinese Characters

中国木偶艺术
Art of Chinese Puppetry

古代兵书
Ancient Books on the Art of War

道教文化
Culture of the Taoism

古代交通
Ancient Transport

古代壁画
Ancient Chinese Mural Painting

古代衡器
Ancient Weighing Apparatus

二十四节气
The Twenty-four Solar Terms

中国名泉
Famous Springs in China

长江黄河
The Yangtze River and the Yellow River

中国杂技
Chinese Acrobatic Art

中国婚俗
Wedding Customs in China

匾额楹联
Inscribed Boards and Couplets

中国建筑装饰
Chinese Architectural Decoration

十二生肖
Chinese Zodiac Signs

古代佩饰
Accessories Wore by Ancient Chinese

文房清供
Stationery and Bibelot in Ancient Studies

中国瑞兽祥禽
Auspicious Animals and Birds in Chinese Culture